PURPOSEFUL

Productivity

MULTIPLY YOUR TIME AND YOUR HAPPINESS

TANYA DALTON

NELSON
BOOKS

An Imprint of Thomas Nelson

Published in Nashville, Tennessee, by Nelson Books, an imprint of Thomas Nelson. Nelson Books and Thomas Nelson are registered trademarks of HarperCollins Christian Publishing, Inc.

Published in association with Yates & Yates, www.yates2.com.

Thomas Nelson titles may be purchased in bulk for educational, business, fund-raising, or sales promotional use. For information, please email SpecialMarkets@ThomasNelson.com.

Any internet addresses, phone numbers, or company or product information printed in this book are offered as a resource and are not intended in any way to be or to imply an endorsement by Thomas Nelson, nor does Thomas Nelson vouch for the existence, content, or services of these sites, phone numbers, companies, or products beyond the life of this book.

All interviews and personal stories are used with permission.

ISBN 978-1-4003-4662-2 (softcover)
ISBN 978-1-4003-4661-5 (ebook)
ISBN 978-1-4003-4663-9 (digital audio)

Library of Congress Cataloging-in-Publication Data is on File

Printed in the United States of America

24 25 26 27 28 LBC 5 4 3 2 1

INTRODUCTION

Have you ever had one of those days where you've run around busy all day long, checking task after task off your to-do list? Where maybe you've crammed 36 hours' worth of activities into a 24-hour day? And yet somehow, at the end of the day, as you slip into bed and your head hits the pillow, you think: *Why didn't I get more done?*

It was that question nagging at me, day after day, that pushed me to first write *The Joy of Missing Out* several years ago. Since that time, I've been amazed and thrilled with the response. I've received so many letters and notes from readers around the world who say things like:

"I feel so much more accomplished and happier."

"I no longer feel like a failure if I don't do everything."

"How did you know how I've secretly been feeling?"

That last one is my favorite because it was repeated in email after email. The truth is: I knew those secret thoughts because I spent years feeling exactly the same. For far too much of my life, I chased busy and pursued perfection until I finally realized I was lusting after everybody else's idea of success.

Maybe you are like me—an overachiever, a people pleaser, a perfecter—so you believe success has been defined by what you do, not who you are. You fill your days in pursuit of this illusion of success, just as I did, but deep down you feel there must be a better way. And you are so right.

It took a hard season in my life to open my eyes and see how we hide behind our busy days and our long lists. We peek out and see that a richer life is available, but we don't feel entitled to it. I'm here to tell you that you deserve that fulfilling life. We can lead extraordinary lives.

We need to change our mindset, though, and redefine what it means to be purposefully productive. *Productivity is not about doing more; it's doing what's most important.* We need to stop trying to get more done and instead reset our focus on our own priorities. When we do that, our ideal lives can become our real, everyday lives.

Throughout this book we will custom design a system that works for you and your life. I want to show you that it's possible to be successful and still focus on your priorities. We don't have to sacrifice one for the other.

Today I help people find more meaning in their lives—professionally and personally—because when I found Purposeful Productivity in my own life, success was inevitable. That's what I want for you.

LET'S GET STARTED

One of the things that truly surprised me most after the release of *The Joy of Missing Out* (JOMO) was how many readers told me that they used the book—almost like a Magic 8 Ball—to set their intention for the day. They would flip through the book, open to a random page, and read a passage. They would use that as their springboard each morning as they planned out their day.

Purposeful Productivity is the book so many of you have asked for—we've taken some of those most loved stories and concepts to create a daily reader. Each chapter includes two thought-provoking questions curated to help you implement and integrate some of those intentions into your day. I want to encourage you to answer the questions honestly. No one else needs to see what you've written, so dive deep into who you are and what you truly want in your life.

To make this even easier—and for those of you who don't want to write in your book—I've created a downloadable question guide you can grab at TanyaDalton.com/purposeful.

Day 1
OVERWHELMED.

It was a beautiful spring morning, but I was too busy to notice the clear blue sky. I was doing my best to keep it all together as I raced the clock, trying to get Kate to preschool drop-off in time. I had a busy day ahead and a to-do list three miles long. With a quick kiss on Kate's cheek, I raced back home, mentally running through all the tasks I needed to do.

I took a step toward my laundry room and stopped. *No, not laundry.* I took a step toward my computer and shook my head. *No, I shouldn't work on that yet.* I turned around and around as I debated what to do first. I literally turned in a circle. The feeling of overwhelm was bubbling up inside of me, making me feel just-this-side of crazy. I crumpled into a heap and cried for a good fifteen minutes.

When I pulled myself up, I was angry at myself. *How could I have wasted time crying?* I said a few choice words to myself about how weak I was and moved on with my day. I buried those emotions deep inside. After all, I had a to-do list to tackle.

Though I didn't know it at the time, I was the cause of my own overwhelm. I was busy being "busy"—filling my day with errands and tasks but never feeling like I'd done enough. It made me feel like I was running in circles, leaving me exhausted. I was busy doing "all the things" so other women would look at me and think I had it all together. But I didn't. Most days started with me wondering how I would possibly keep up this facade and ended with me feeling like a failure.

I was living my days in this constant state of overwhelm.

Overwhelmed.

This is the word I hear from so many when they describe how they feel about their days. Overwhelmed by their responsibilities. Overwhelmed by their own to-do lists. Overwhelmingly overwhelmed.

Here's some truth I want to share with you: Overwhelm isn't having too much to do; it's not knowing where to start.

But knowing where to begin can be incredibly difficult. Real productivity helps us know where to start. It's intentionally choosing to cut through the clutter and noise in our lives. It's discovering the happiness that comes when we center our lives on what is truly important to us and let go of the rest.

1. What do you think of Tanya's definition of overwhelm: "Overwhelm isn't having too much to do: it's not knowing where to start"? Do you agree or disagree with this idea?

2. How do you feel when you don't know what to work on next or where to begin your day?

3. What does being productive mean to you? Does productive mean getting a lot of tasks crossed off your to-do list, or does it mean doing work that satisfies you? How do you think your idea of productivity might change after reading this book?

Day 2

WHAT DID YOU DO TODAY?

What did you do today?"

The question was posed innocently enough, in between bites of dinner. I was leaning across the table, cutting Jack's chicken into tiny pieces, and I felt the knife skitter across the plate like a record skipping.

I knew John was genuinely interested in how I'd spent my day. But every evening when he asked me that question, I would sense my heartbeat quickening ever so slightly.

I hated that question.

I hated it because it made me feel small. It made me feel like I needed to justify how I'd spent the last twelve hours of my day—not to him, but to myself. I thought I needed to prove I had spent my day being the best worker, the best mom, the best friend, the best . . . well, everything.

And yet I always fell a little short. Not quite there. I believed I hadn't worked hard enough or long enough, I hadn't crossed off enough items on my list, or I hadn't been patient enough and had fussed at the kids too much.

It didn't matter that I had run myself ragged all day long.

Quite honestly, most nights when the question was posed, my mind went absolutely blank like a chalkboard wiped clean. What had I done all day? When I frantically scoured the edges of my brain, I overlooked the multitude of jobs I had fulfilled throughout my day: mother, business owner, friend. The list went on and on.

If I had paused and taken a deep breath, I would have remembered I had answered a solid handful of customer emails, taken the kids to the library, used the in-between moments to toss loads of laundry, and made some serious progress on my new website. I would have given myself the grace to see what everyone else around me saw: a woman who was doing her very best.

But I couldn't see it. Instead of sharing all my wins, I rattled off what I hadn't done. I forgot to sign up Jack for art class; I didn't get a chance to stop at the post office; I wasn't able to finish with the blog post; and—

"Wow," John cut in jokingly, "didn't you do anything right today?"

Hot tears streamed down my face because I could not see a single thing I'd done "right." Always falling a little short. I was good about seeing the good in others, but never in myself.

1. Do you think you connect your self-worth to how busy you are throughout your day?
2. Do you give more grace to others than you do yourself? Why do you think that is?

Day 3

MARBLE JAR MOMENTS

Are you familiar with the marble jar trick? It's an old tactic teachers have used forever. I used it myself in my years when I stood at the front of a classroom. It's simple, really—every time the kids do something good, you drop a marble in a jar. When the jar fills up, well, that's when the class gets a reward.

But it's not just the reward that's exciting. That fresh marble makes a solid, satisfying clink as it bounces around in the jar. The kids' eyes get big and round when you hold up the marble, and they quiet down just to hear it rattle its way into the jar.

For the years I taught, I was a big believer in the power of the marble jar, and with great reason—it reinforces good work. We want credit for all the good we've done, which is why I believe we all have an invisible marble jar we carry around with us, begging to be filled.

Got up and worked out . . . marble in the jar! Made the kids' lunch . . . marble in the jar—wait, it was a *healthy* lunch . . . *two* marbles in the jar! And so, our day continues with marbles clinking and filling up our jars.

The problem with these imaginary jars comes when something doesn't go quite right. We forget an important ingredient for dinner, or we miss a deadline at work, and we don't just say, "Oops! No marble in the jar." We feel so defeated that we loosen our grip and allow our jar to slip out of our hands and crash onto the floor.

Marbles and broken glass are everywhere. It doesn't matter that the jar was almost full. It doesn't matter that we had done really well. Instead of picking up those perfectly good marbles we earned, we decide we need to hustle to earn more marbles. We overfill our schedules with tasks and errands, desperately trying to refill our jars, which seem to shatter again and again throughout our day.

Our days are filled with far too many of these marble jar moments. We have to make it stop.

But too many of us tie our self-worth to our busyness. Stress and overwhelm are badges of honor declaring our worthiness. *We falsely believe that if we are* not *busy, we are failing.* In the pursuit of finding balance, we try to do everything, but the more we do, the less we succeed.

1. What marbles did you put into your jar today?
2. Which mistakes are you allowing to outweigh your successes today?

Day 4

WHAT ARE YOUR STORIES?

We all have a library of folklore filled with stories about ourselves that we believe. We need to ask ourselves, *Are these stories even true?*

Over time we all accumulate beliefs about ourselves and about life. These stories we repeatedly tell ourselves gain a mythology-like quality and begin to feel like truth. Often these stories are steeped in other people's truths—in their ideas and opinions that we've gathered together and made our own.

We hold ourselves up to the high standards these stories demand, even when they aren't realistic. These stories are almost always written in absolutes, using the words *always* and *never*:

A good mom never hires a babysitter to give herself some alone time.
A good friend always returns a text within ten minutes.
A good boss never leaves work before anyone else on the team.

Are these statements true? Are they fair? We set ourselves up for unrealistic expectations no one could achieve, and, in fact, we wouldn't hold *anyone else* to these standards. These stories transform into limiting beliefs that hold us back; they demand that we spend our time in ways that don't *really* fit the life we want. We follow their strict rules because we think we should. We think we are supposed to behave a certain way, and so we do.

One of the stories I told myself for years was that good moms stay home. They have cookies baked when their kids get off the bus, and they volunteer almost daily at their kids' school. That's what my mom did, so I set those requirements for myself.

But those rules didn't work for me, which made me feel guilty because I believed I *should have been* fulfilled by those things—but I wasn't. I *really* like working, and my work schedule made it hard to fulfill these strict requirements I had set for myself. I couldn't let go of the guilt that was telling me I wasn't a good mom. It ate away at me and my happiness. I had to change my thinking: I don't stay at home, but I make a conscious effort to be there in the afternoons to help with homework.

I quieted the stories in my head and reset my expectations to make them realistic for my life. I do what I can, and my story now tells me: *A good mom loves her children the best she can.*

1. Are there stories you're telling yourself about the "right" way you should be living?
2. How can you rewrite those *always/never* stories so you can live a happier life?

Day 5

YOUR UNKNOWN STRENGTH

We've all heard tales of people who suddenly acquire super-human strength to lift a car when a child is trapped beneath or who heave huge slabs of concrete rubble aside after an earth-quake. While not all of us may experience a surge in adrenaline like that, we all have a superhuman ability inside us to transform.

In early October 2009, eighty-seven-year-old Warren climbed on the roof of his home to make a quick repair. One week later, he was diagnosed with a cancer so severe that by Thanksgiving his family was carrying out the mournful task of planning his funeral. His widow, Gwen, was suddenly on her own.

Gwen had never lived alone—at the age of eighteen, she had moved from her parents' house directly into her new husband's home. She had never paid an electric bill or pumped her own gas. With Warren's death, her family fretted about how Gwen would hold up, but Gwen surprised them all.

When talk came up after the funeral about her moving, she put her foot down and insisted she would live alone in the home she had built with Warren. And she did. She made adjustments and created a whole new independent life for herself.

Gwen didn't just survive—she thrived. Why? Because, at the age of eighty-three, she was willing to understand she had other roles to live. She wasn't just a widow—she was a mother, a grandmother, a pie baker, a friend. She took on a new role as encourager for the elderly. She had a regular rotation of visits to women in the nursing homes—a group she lovingly referred to as "my old ladies." And now Gwen is gunning for one hundred because, in her own words, she has a lot to live for. I know this because Gwen happens to be my grandma.

She had a strength inside her no one knew about. In fact, *she* didn't even know this strength existed. She didn't allow herself to be defined by her eighty-three years of being dependent on someone else.

Sometimes we have to let go of our old stories.

1. Put yourself in Gwen's shoes—you've had a life experience that has taken you completely outside any comfort zone you've ever had. How do you think you'd respond?
2. What strengths do you suspect are hiding within you that have simply never been tested?

Day 6
CHANGE YOUR CONJUNCTION

I've met thousands of people through speaking and workshops, and many have shared with me that they identify closely with one role. It defines every part of who they are, which leaves almost no room for anything else—certainly no room for other priorities or dreams that fall outside these tight parameters. I hear stories like these:

> *I can be a mom* OR *I can chase my dream of opening my business.*
> *I can be a career woman* OR *a hands-on parent.*
> *I can take care of my elderly parents* OR *pursue my art career.*

They fool themselves with their stories and conclude that life is an either/or situation.

When we spend a long time centered on one role, we often find it hard to look around and see other possibilities. A slight change to your conjunction will do it: A fantastic parent *and* an entrepreneur. An artist *and* a caregiver. A hands-on mom *and* a career woman?

But let me be clear: This is not about piling more on our

plates—it's about shifting the way we look at who we are and reclaiming our lives by placing what's important to us front and center.

Far too many of us have pushed aside our aspirations because we believe we don't have time or don't have the right to pursue them. This is just another story we need to reset.

Are you ready to effect some change in your life even with the possibility of experiencing discomfort? Because change is a disruption; it's something people tend to avoid—even if it means staying on the same old path heading in a direction they don't really love.

I'll be honest. I know that sticking with the status quo is easier. After all, it's a well-worn path—we know where it turns, where the rocks are . . . but do you like where it's heading? The road to change is full of uncertainty, so it can be scary. But we need some discomfort to make a change.

When we are doing something new, we are shifting our mindset. And that means something fulfilling is just around the corner.

1. Is there a single role that you feel you've identified strongly with in the past?
2. If you changed your conjunction, how would you describe yourself? Fill in the blanks: As a _____ and a _____.

OWN IT

Today I want you to make a choice:

    a. I will choose my own path and priorities.
    b. I will let others choose my path and priorities.

If you chose *B*, you might want to stop and put the book down. You won't like the rest of this book—because I believe we all want and need to be in charge of our choices. This is hard, though, especially when so many people believe they don't have ownership over their day.

Too often we hand over the reins, allowing others to imprison us with their own agendas and urgent fires that need putting out. We've simply forgotten that we have the ability to choose to spend time on our own priorities.

We all know what a priority is—it's something that is important to us. But the struggle for most people is understanding what is a priority and what isn't. After all, how can we prioritize when *everything* feels important?

When we treat everything as equal, it means nothing is a

priority. It all gets jumbled together, and we begin to lose sight of what really matters. We believe we should be able to exhaust all the opportunities available. Because we don't want to miss out on anything, we treat everything as if it's important—even when it's not. This leaves us feeling like a dog chasing its tail.

In reality no one needs #allthethings, just the things that are truly fulfilling *to them*. It's hard to let things go, especially when there's a little bit of safety or comfort involved. Focusing your time, getting rid of some of the noise, and lasering in on your priorities sometimes takes some discomfort. I know this myself firsthand.

We need to discover the priorities that are unique to us, but first we have to take hold of this truth: *We must be willing to not have it all.*

1. Look at your to-do list for today. How many of those items are really *your* priorities?
2. Does the idea of "not having it all" spark fear or inspiration? Why?

Day 8

IS IT TOO LATE TO CHANGE?

October in Asheville, North Carolina, is gorgeous. The weather dips into the cool temperatures of fall, and the mountains start to light up in brilliant oranges and reds. It's one of my favorite times of the year—every year except 2013.

I had started my own business years earlier, and I had grown it to the point where John could leave the corporate world and work alongside me. We worked shoulder to shoulder, putting our all into the business, and I loved working together. And yet, I wasn't happy. I felt a deep, nagging sense of dissatisfaction.

I couldn't put my finger on what it was—I just knew I felt weighted down and heavy with the burden of waking up to a job that didn't really tick the boxes of what was important to me. I was spending my days spinning my wheels, chasing after a life that made me feel exhausted and empty.

Most of my days ended with me feeling defeated and unfulfilled because I didn't love what I was putting forth into the world. And that unhappiness with my work was making me feel hollow. My business, though, was the sole income for our family—it allowed us to live.

I owed that business a lot, but I dreamed of finding a life where I could feel full again and satisfied with my work. How could I possibly turn my back on a thriving business that paid my family's bills to pursue something new? A feeling of powerlessness loomed over me like a dark cloud.

I felt stuck. It seemed obvious to me that there were no other options.

You may have experienced this feeling yourself. In fact, while reading this book, you may have thought to yourself, *That sounds nice, but there's no way I can make that happen in my life*, or *I would love to spend time on my personal priorities, but there's just too much to do.*

Let me lay a little tough love on you right now that I had to learn too: *You can choose or let others choose for you. The choice is really yours.* Not making a choice *is* a choice.

1. Have you ever been in a situation where you felt you had no choice? How did that make you feel?
2. In times when you've opted not to make a choice, what has been the result? What regrets did you have?

Day 9

THE TRUTH ABOUT CHOICES

Have you ever experienced that feeling of having no control over your day? As if your world is so rigid and made up of so many rules you don't really get to choose the life you live? That, my friend, is learned helplessness. That feeling of being stuck (and that I didn't want to think about how empty I felt)? That was my own learned helplessness rearing its ugly head.

Learned helplessness can lead us to overlook opportunities for relief. A good example of this is when a student studies for a test and yet still performs poorly. When it's time to study for the next test, she may believe there's no point because "she won't do well anyway," so she doesn't bother.

She forgets that for the first test, she went out late the night before. She only remembers that she studied and didn't do well; therefore, studying didn't help. She feels stuck and doesn't see any other choice, so she simply stops trying.

It's not reality that makes us feel stuck; it's the lens we use to view the world. Maybe you are tired of trying because it feels like it just doesn't seem to matter. I've felt this way too. There are times when we all just want to crawl back in bed and throw the covers over our heads because we are so overwhelmed with the chaotic rush of our days.

We can lose sight of who we are deep inside and what is most important to us. We are so busy struggling and fighting to keep our heads above water that we forget we can choose to tread water for a moment. We can allow ourselves a deep breath—we can choose to swim to calmer waters.

When we gift ourselves with the ability to step back and choose, something powerful begins to happen. We strengthen our internal locus of control. In other words, we remember we have the ability to influence our own destiny instead of allowing the current to push us wherever it wants.

People with a strong internal locus of control believe they have the freedom and ability to make their own choices and determine what happens to them. Because of that, they are significantly happier and more motivated. Psychologists have found that an "internal locus of control has been linked with academic success . . . higher self-motivation and social maturity . . . lower incidences of stress and depression . . . and longer life span." We want to strengthen our internal locus of control and begin to understand that we have choices.

1. Do you ever feel like you have no control over your time? Do you think this is true, or is it a form of learned helplessness?

2. Think of a situation in your life where you feel like you don't have a choice. What are two ways you could push back or try a different approach that might help you discover some additional solutions?

Day 10

GRAB YOUR SLEDGEHAMMER

During that dark October in 2013, I remember looking out my back window and watching the wind whip past while leaves settled on our worn-out deck. It looked just as tired as I felt, so I grabbed a sledgehammer to start tearing it down.

Projects involving building and power tools are some of the things in life I truly enjoy. I wanted to rebuild that deck, but even more so, I wanted to see if I still had any fire left inside me. I was scared I no longer had the ability to feel the satisfaction I craved. Twenty minutes later, John appeared by my side with a hammer in hand. As with all things, we were in this together.

There we were, silently swinging and sweating side by side, tearing away the old pieces of wood, and it felt *great*. Not good, not okay—I felt alive. We worked on that deck while the weather changed from cool to downright cold; I stepped back after a solid week of hard work and saw the structure we had created. I knew right then that we would be okay. There was still drive and passion inside me. I could still build something new.

In that moment, I had no idea what that "something new" would be, but I knew I couldn't keep slogging through my days feeling numb. I understood I needed to discover what was at the heart of what I wanted to do. I have to be honest and admit this uncertainty was scary, but the idea of continuing on the same path I was on was even scarier. I didn't want to waste any more time living an unfulfilled life. We have a limited amount of time in our lives, so it's important to spend it on the things that matter most.

1. If you're being honest with yourself, what part of your life could use a sledgehammer to make room for something new and more fulfilling?

2. What passion projects and dreams are still alive but maybe have just been buried or numbed?

WHAT ARE YOUR REGRETS?

Bronnie Ware knew she wanted to help others. She found a job working as a palliative care nurse, a job that really suited her. She was a great caretaker and even better listener, both of which are key traits when caring for the seriously ill.

She listened to her patients' stories and memories, and within the first year she began to notice a pattern emerging. Regret. Regret for a lifetime of choices:

> *I wish I'd had the courage to live life true to myself, not the life others expected of me.*
> *I wish I hadn't worked so hard.*
> *I wish I'd had the courage to express my feelings.*
> *I wish I'd stayed in touch with my friends.*
> *I wish I'd let myself be happier.*

That last one gets me the most—*I wish I'd let myself be happier.* I think the thing that stands out to me is the phrase "let myself." Why *don't* we allow ourselves to be happy, to become the people we want to be?

"Isn't it selfish to think of your own priorities?" I've had some people ask. When you become the person you want to be, this not only enhances your own life but benefits the lives of everyone around you.

If I'm guessing, I'd say family and friends are at the top of your priorities. Maybe it's tied to creating a better life or perhaps a goal you haven't pursued. Those priorities, are they just for you? Or are they about cultivating relationships, providing security for those you care about, and maybe even creating an impact in the world around you?

That's not selfish. That's life-giving. It's not selfish to live a fulfilling, happy life, but we often wrestle with feeling guilty about enjoying our time.

Happiness is not a limited resource. You are not going to use it all up. If anything, it's a resource that exponentially grows when it's cultivated. Happiness spreads.

Your happiness isn't defined by others, it is defined by you and the daily choices you make. Living a life centered on your priorities is making a choice to be happy, and it's okay to choose happy.

1. Do you think you let yourself be happy? Or are there times where you don't allow yourself to fully enjoy the moment? Why do you think that is?

2. As you think about your life choices so far, is there anything you regret not doing? Is there a way to use that?

WHO DO YOU WANT TO BE?

I magine this: You are sitting at your kitchen table on a beautiful spring morning. You leisurely munch on your toast while you scroll your phone for the morning's news. Suddenly your eyes widen as you spy your own name on the screen—an announcement of your death.

While this may seem far-fetched, this little fiction is based on the true story of Alfred Nobel, a scientist credited with around 355 inventions. His most notable was a stable explosive to replace the highly volatile (and very dangerous) nitroglycerin. Alfred named his invention "dynamite."

Alfred felt secure about his legacy, but that changed in 1888 when his brother Ludvig died while in France. Instead of publishing Ludvig's obituary, however, the newspaper mistakenly wrote: "Dr. Alfred Nobel, who became rich by finding ways to kill more people faster than ever before, died yesterday." The article was titled "The Merchant of Death Is Dead."[1]

Yikes. There's a headline that would make you spit out your toast.

Alfred had believed dynamite was a gift to humanity, as it made working conditions safer for thousands. To see printed in black and white that this was not how he was perceived devastated him. Provoked by this event and disappointed by how he would be remembered, Nobel set out to change his legacy. He set aside the bulk of his estate to establish prizes to honor men and women for outstanding achievements in physics, chemistry, medicine, literature, and in working toward peace. The Nobel Prize became an extension of his clearer focus.

When he did die in 1896, he was remembered as a humanitarian and an advocate for the sciences, certainly not as a merchant of death. He had made a conscious choice to redirect his life and to create his own legacy.

1. How do you want your friends and family to describe you? Does that desire help you begin to identify your priorities?
2. If Nobel's experience happened to you today, what would the article say about your legacy? How do you actually want to be remembered?

FINDING YOUR WAY

The North Star has long been known as a constant in the night sky. Throughout history, it has guided sailors and adventurers on the path to their ultimate destinations, keeping them from being lost long before there were maps. The North Star is the beacon shining through the dark unknown, lighting our path.

While we may not be sailors, we still need a constant in our life to help guide us through the darkness. Here's the hard fact: *We don't just find ourselves on a fulfilling, deeply satisfying path—we create it for ourselves.* The clarity comes from within us.

Our purpose and our priorities need to drive our productivity. The more we allow our North Star to guide us, the more productive and fulfilled we will become. *When we live our life using our North Star, we take ownership of our legacy.*

When we don't define our North Star, we allow others to define it for us. And often this means we are spending time being busy instead of focusing on moving forward in the direction we truly want to go. Our North Star determines how we want to spend our time and, most importantly, guides our decisions.

I want you to think about this: How many times a week, or

even a day, do you make decisions? Even those small decisions you aren't actively thinking about, like scrolling through your phone instead of engaging in conversation with your loved ones. We forget we are actively making those choices. Having a North Star guides you in your daily life and drives the direction of your choices—big and small.

Decisions become easier when we have this foundation of confidence. At its core, *productivity is about making a series of choices.* Choices have the power to make us genuinely productive rather than simply busy. By not making choices and allowing others' priorities to become our own, we will never feel truly productive, no matter how many tasks we check off our lists. We have to sort through the opportunities and activities and choose to focus on what's most important.

1. Identify three small decisions you made yesterday without thinking, where maybe you were simply being busy rather than truly productive. List them here.
2. If you could spend today doing anything you wanted, how would you spend it?

DISCOVER YOUR NORTH STAR

Earlier I shared that when I was tearing apart my deck that I felt lost and realized I needed to discover my North Star. I remember going online and searching for answers. I knew my current path wasn't the right one for me, but what *was* the right path? Every article I found began with the phrase "Start by writing down your purpose." I wanted to scream at the computer because that was the problem—I had no idea.

I knew there was a path that was destined for me, but it had become so overrun with weeds I could no longer see it. I felt lost. At times I would literally imagine myself alone in an overgrown woods, turning in circles with no idea of where to step next. I was scared. Scared to move and scared to stand still.

I didn't really know what my North Star was—I had to discover it for myself. And I think that's one of the most important parts of the process: ownership. You have to take this journey; you have to do the work because this is *your* path. The good, the bad, and the ugly: *It belongs to you. So, own it.*

Our North Star is a combination of our mission, vision statement, and core values. Each one answers the question of who you are at your heart. The mission statement tells us what we are doing now, the vision statement tells of where we want to be, and the core values tell us how these can be defined through our actions. Like pieces of a puzzle, they come together to create the completed picture of why we make the choices we do. They become the North Star we need to guide us through decisions.

I cannot design this North Star for you; neither can your best friend or your family. Your North Star is uniquely yours. It's your own filter for guiding your behavior and choices providing clear guidance to make the best decisions to help you achieve your goals. It's important to take the time to custom design it for yourself.

1. What do you like most about yourself and where you're heading with your life?
2. What words would you use to describe your personal values and beliefs?

Day 15

SHAKE IT UP

Some people find terms like *mission statement* and *core values* intimidating. It's almost like the words themselves are heavy because they feel so important. I think many people believe these words work to define them—now, always, and forever. This idea is what causes a huge stumbling block—no wonder it feels so heavy! Yes, they do add value and structure to our lives, but the process doesn't have to be intimidating or frightening.

We are constantly evolving, learning, and growing. We are in a constant state of change, so why would we assume our values and priorities are fixed? Take a minute and think of who you were just two years ago. What were you doing, how did you define yourself, and what was important to you at the time? You have changed (and will continue to change). So will your North Star. It grows and evolves with you, which is why it's important to take time often to think about the components of your North Star and ask yourself, *Does it reflect me and where I want to go now?* It's okay if it doesn't. It just means it's time to shake things up a little, or maybe even a lot.

Just take a deep breath and don't overthink it.

1. Write down your answers to the questions in the passage about who you were just two years ago—what you were doing, how you defined yourself, and what was important to you at the time.

2. Based on who you are now, to what extent does how you're living reflect where you're wanting to go? What do you need to leave behind? What could use some shaking up?

Day 16
YOUR MISSION

Your mission statement answers the question: "What do I do?" It should be true to you and specific enough for people to understand what you do and why you do it. Many people and companies get this wrong by using big fancy words that don't tell us anything. *Clear and concise* is the name of the game. We want our mission statement to be easy to memorize and repeat because we will be referencing it often.

Here are some examples of mission statements:

Amazon: To be Earth's most customer-centric company, Earth's best employer, and Earth's safest place to work.

Nike: To bring inspiration and innovation to every athlete in the world.

PBS: To use media to educate, inspire, entertain, and express a diversity of perspectives.

inkWELL Press (my company): To provide productivity tools and trainings that empower you to achieve your goals and dreams.

Do you see how these mission statements allow them to make decisions about their movements and their choices? Their statements are not about the *things* they do—Nike doesn't tell you they make athletic gear, and PBS doesn't talk about producing great children's programs. Instead, a mission statement gets to the heart of why they do these things.

When it comes to your mission statement, maybe the question you should be asking isn't "What do I do?" but it should dig deeper and ask, "*Why* do I do what I do?"

You can see how a mission statement helps these companies determine what they spend their resources on—and what they don't. Even though you're not a company, you too are inundated with choices. And while you aren't offering a product or service, you are crafting a legacy—that's your ultimate product, the impact you make for yourself and others.

We all have gifts; there's a feeling of satisfaction when you focus your time and energy on what is truly at the heart of what you do. Writing a mission statement for yourself gives you that clarity.

1. Remember that your mission is your *why*, not your *what*. And it centers on the impact you want to make for yourself and others. So, list out several things you love to do and then ask yourself: *Why* do I love each of these things? Why does it bring me joy?

2. What clues or key words do you find in what you just wrote that might be building blocks for your mission statement?

SO MANY HATS

My personal mission statement is: "To use my passion and expertise in productivity to inspire others to achieve their goals and dreams." Notice I don't mention the words *business owner* or *author* or *podcaster*. It's a short statement that conveys what I do and why.

One of the beauties of a mission statement is that it helps guide and remind you of what you do, but it doesn't box you in. It provides the framework you use to make your decisions. When it's time for me to decide whether to say yes to a project or whether to join a committee, the proposal must first filter through my mission statement. I ask myself, *Does this fulfill my mission?* If it does, I move forward. If something doesn't fit my mission, the answer is a clear and simple no. My mission statement has given me the insight to know what I really want to focus on every day.

I think one of the struggles many people experience with an exercise like this is that it's hard to zero in on one statement. We have so many facets to our lives, we cannot imagine a single statement being able to convey it all. I'll give you an example of what I mean by this.

Amanda is a woman with a lot on her plate. She homeschools her three daughters, teaches high school English at her co-op, works part-time as a physical therapist, *and* works on her dream business on the side as a professional organizer.

She wears so many hats, she wasn't sure where to laser in on her mission statement. But I noticed a key thread running through each of her activities: She is consistently spreading love and helping others in many different forms. When we focused on the root of *why* she does each of these tasks, she said she is passionate about helping others overcome challenges, "inviting them to walk in hope, empowerment, and freedom." Once she acknowledged this, Amanda was able to create a mission statement she felt reflected her many hats. So can you.

1. Are you like Amanda, wearing a lot of hats? Which hats do you wear most consistently?

2. In thinking about all the hats you wear, is there a key thread among them?

CREATING THE VISION

A vision statement answers the question: "Where am I going?" It's where we dream we will be. This may be very different from where we are right now. It helps set our trajectory and define where the destination lies. A vision statement is not your goals—it's a description of your future that instills hope. It's not the nitty-gritty details of each step required to get there; it's a guideline to help you understand the goals you may need to set. One of the best parts of a vision statement is that it's not necessarily tied to your current reality. It's an opportunity to imagine the best possible future.

Some examples of focused vision statements:

Make-A-Wish: To grant the wish of every eligible child.
Avon: To be the company that best understands and satisfies the product, service and self-fulfillment needs of women—globally.
ASPCA: That animals in the United States live good lives; valued by society, protected by its laws and free from cruelty, pain, and suffering.

inkWELL Press: To help people everywhere live a fulfilling life focusing on their priorities.

Did you notice that these are written in absolute terms? You don't see phrases like "hope to be" or "would like to have." They are written as if these statements will absolutely come true.

Because a vision statement is meant to be used internally, many companies don't publish theirs for the public to see. Most people follow this as well; it's really designed to be a more personal statement. I'm happy to share mine, though: "I will help people everywhere live a fulfilling life, focusing on their priorities while focusing on my own."

One of the most powerful exercises I used when designing my vision statement was to create a vision board. Simply gather a pile of magazines you don't mind cutting up and start flipping. Look for images and words that inspire you. When something jumps out at you, rip it out. And then keep flipping.

Once you have a nice stack, intentionally choose whichever items represent the vision of the future you want. Attach the images on a large sheet of paper or poster board, something you can hang in a place where you'll see it often. Then use the ideas you've gathered to craft a meaningful vision statement for yourself.

1. When you dream of the future, what do you want your life to look like? What vision do you see for yourself?
2. What are some words or phrases you would like to put on your vision board?

COMPLETING YOUR NORTH STAR

Core values answer the question: "How will I support the mission and vision statements?" Your core values work in concert with your vision and mission statements to create the essential standards that guide your behavior and shape your decisions.

Start collecting the values that come to mind. It may help to look at a list of common words used for core values—I have a list at tanyadalton.com/purposeful. Use a highlighter to go through and choose what resonates with you.

You will at this point have a good-sized list of values, but you don't want too many. Six or fewer is a good rule of thumb here: enough to stand for something, but not so many you feel like you're juggling chain saws. To refine your list, look for ways you can group the words together into categories or themes, then choose a label that embodies the full idea. For example, when I was doing this exercise for myself, I grouped together *authentic, generosity, kindness, thoughtfulness*, and *charity* and ended up naming that value "Grace."

Now start actively working to incorporate your values into your daily life and decision-making. If you live focused on your values, people will see them from the actions you take and the words you speak. Your core values fulfill the prophecy of your mission and vision statements and create structure for the life you want to live.

The process of defining your North Star might seem daunting, but when we design a life where our mission, vision, and core values are an integral part, we have a guide to help us with the overwhelm we may have been feeling. A good North Star guides you to know what decisions to make and how to start.

1. Let's bring everything together*:
My Mission Statement

My Vision Statement

My Core Values

*It's okay if you still aren't fully sold on each of them. Write down what you have right now and then come back later and refine.

2. How does this feel to have a North Star?

Day 20
WHERE THE MAGIC HAPPENS

The idea of doing it all—and doing it well—is the problem I have with the concept of balance. Balance sounds nice, but it's nothing more than a productivity buzzword, an empty promise that leads us to falsely believe we should be able to do everything equally.

If life is perfectly balanced, we aren't really moving forward; instead, we are spinning chaotically like a top. We can take charge of our destinies only when we let go of balance and decide the direction we want our lives to go. Movement, in any direction, requires shifting—it requires counterbalance.

Think about balance like riding a bike. A bike has the ability to move in a deliberate direction. It requires some equilibrium to stay upright, but have you ever tried to balance on a bike that's perfectly still? It's almost impossible. We have to lean forward a bit and start gathering momentum by pushing on the pedals. The energy we create keeps us from falling over.

With a bike, we can choose to turn and move along a path we really want. We can go left or right by shifting our balance— we have to move away from perfect balance in order to turn. If we continue to lean heavily to the side, though, we will topple over. We need to counterbalance, readjusting our center of gravity to keep the bike upright and moving forward on this new path.

You see, *magic doesn't happen when life is centered and balanced—it happens when we lean into our priorities.* Have you ever thought about that? When we start concentrating on what is truly important to us, we *will* go out of balance. Imbalance is instrumental in making us purposefully productive.

1. What are your concerns at the thought of going out of balance? How does the idea of intentionally going out of balance make you feel? Why?

2. How does it feel to realize that, like a bike, your life moves forward as you shift your balance? Remind yourself, *I can do this!*

Day 21

THE ILLUSION OF BALANCE

Creating an extraordinary life for ourselves actually requires letting go of the concept of balance. When we lean into a priority—when we give time to the most important things—we have to take that time away from something else. We cannot give equal time to all the tasks on our lists.

Let me explain. We all have three key resources available to share with the world—*time*, *energy*, and *focus*. Each of these elements, though, is a depleting commodity; once it's invested, it's gone forever. You cannot get it back. By far, these are the most valuable resources we have to give.

While we are all different, our lives are made up of the same three buckets that need to be filled: work, home, and personal. The problem is, we believe we need to distribute our time, energy, and focus in each of these areas evenly. But it's simply not possible.

In an effort to make these buckets feel like they are somewhat even, we spread our resources far and wide, making little to no impact. We end up stretching ourselves thin.

In chasing the illusion of balance, we end up creating a life that feels busy—not meaningful. We have to be willing to go out of balance. We need to be willing *not* to do everything.

When we combine the three resources of time, energy, and focus, though, we'll discover exceptional results. This is true in all the areas of our lives, including our relationships, our work, and, yes, our productivity. We need all three to work united together to make the biggest impact possible in our days.

1. Are there a few areas of your life where you might have unintentionally created "a life that feels busy—not meaningful"?

2. What would a "meaningful life" look like for you?

GOOD, BETTER, BEST

For too long, I had no idea where to spend my time or how to spend my energy. I wasn't productive—I was simply running around being busy, filling my days but not my soul. I was lacking focus, one of the key elements of true productivity that allows us to choose how we spend our day.

To be genuinely productive, we must master our focus. That can feel difficult, I know. We are pulled in a thousand different directions through the pings on our phones, the blips of our inboxes, and the endless opportunities we have before us. In our digital age, we have more information at our fingertips than ever before in history. We have watches that tell us our heart rate and apps that tell us precisely what time we should expect rain this evening. We have alerts on our phones to tell us about traffic and more access to news than we ever even thought we wanted.

It seems like this abundance of information should make life easier, but when we are bombarded with so much of it, the paradox is that decision-making becomes more difficult. This is when the feeling of overwhelm begins to settle in and we simply don't know where to start.

We receive approximately eleven million pieces of information every second from our nerve endings, but our brains can only process a mere fifty bits.[2] There seems to be no easy way to wade through the information and choose where to focus, so our natural reaction is simply to stop filtering. We choose not to choose.

We have to become comfortable with some doubt because oftentimes the problem isn't discerning between good and bad—the black and white—it's choosing between two good choices. It's when the black and white blends into gray. It's the good, better, and best—how do you decide where to focus?

I received a letter from Amanda in Salem, South Dakota, who described this dilemma well:

> I have all these thoughts and ideas . . . but I STRUGGLE in the action portion. I feel like this massive paralysis comes over me when I actually need to put ideas to work. I feel like I don't know where to start in getting my life organized to better enjoy my family and work.

Amanda is not alone in feeling this way—and neither are you.

1. How would you rate your current degree of focus?

CONSTANTLY PINBALLING ☆ ☆ ☆ ☆ ☆ ☆ ☆ ☆ ☆ ☆ CLEAR & SHARP

2. Do you ever feel the same way as Amanda? What do you do when you start feeling overwhelmed?

Day 23

BURN THE BOATS

Archimedes was a Greek mathematician and inventor in ancient Syracuse. There are many anecdotes about Archimedes, but the legend of his defense of his hometown against the onslaught of conquering Romans is one of my favorites.

Archimedes knew his countrymen were far outnumbered and did not have the sophisticated weaponry needed to defend their coast, so he devised a simple weapon constructed solely of mirrors, which he placed high on the cliffs. This effective tool did one job: It reflected the rays of the sun. Directing the rays toward the oncoming boats, he was able to ignite every enemy ship before it reached the shoreline, keeping his country safe. What's important to note is that it wasn't the sun alone that protected the coast—it was the focus of the sun's energy.

As Alexander Graham Bell once said, "Concentrate all your thought upon the work at hand. The sun's rays do not burn until brought to a focus."[3] It's not about creating a huge effort; it's about focusing like a magnifying glass in order to burn the boats.

One way to help ignite that fire is by setting goals. Similar to Archimedes's mirror, goals focus our energy into a powerful motivator. Goals, when done correctly, are the magnifying glass we need to concentrate our energy and sharpen our focus. They help us weed through all the information and center in on the steps we want to take to move ourselves forward.

This is key in moving us along the path our North Star is guiding us toward. Goals are an extension of the foundation we have created, and they help shape our choices to get us to the end result we want.

1. What kinds of distractions do you deal with on a regular basis?
2. What can you do to eliminate these distractions?

Day 24
POWER GOALS

If you are anything like most people, you may find yourself questioning whether goal setting really works (especially if it hasn't for you in the past), but I'll share a study[4] that shows the power of setting goals.

Researchers studied Harvard MBA students before graduation and asked them, "Have you set clear, written goals for your future and made plans to accomplish them?" They found that 84 percent of students had no goals set, 13 percent had goals in mind but didn't write them down, and only 3 percent had goals written on paper along with clear plans to accomplish them.

Ten years passed, and the researchers checked back in with the graduates and discovered that the abstract goal setters were making twice the amount of money as the students who had set no goals. Impressive, right? But the real success story was in the 3 percent who had written their goals; they were taking home ten times the amount of the other 97 percent *combined*.

Why does setting goals help? Because it helps us clarify what we want to accomplish. In other words, it tells us where to focus. It enables us to clearly see the path we want to take and triggers our behavior. When we set a goal, it naturally directs our focus to where we want to expend our energy and our time.

Without goals, how do you know the trajectory of your path? Goals tell us exactly where to aim. As Zig Ziglar said, "If you aim at nothing, you'll hit it every time." We have the power to burn boats if we stay focused.

When we lose focus on our priorities, we are simply along for the ride, going wherever the day takes us. The act of focusing is that—an act. It's a verb rather than a noun. And this focus requires making choices. Choices may feel difficult, because when we eliminate options, we feel that we are limiting ourselves, but in reality, that's what allows us the freedom to live the life we really want.

1. If you had been part of the Harvard goal-setting study, which group would you have been in?
2. How do you feel about writing your goals after reading the results of the study?

Day 25

BOUNDARIES CREATE FREEDOM

We have to cut in order to really grow and flourish. I know this seems counterintuitive, but think of a garden: Do you plant the flowers one on top of another? Do you squeeze so many in that there is no room? Or do you allow each plant to have space— space to receive the rain and the sun, space to spread their leaves and grow? That's what we need: space to allow ourselves to focus. The only way to have that space is to actively create it for ourselves. We need boundaries.

Often we hear a word like boundaries and believe that we are limiting ourselves and our choices. What we don't realize is that boundaries are actually a source of freedom. Solid boundaries allow us that space we need to focus.

When we compartmentalize, we give ourselves that space and freedom.

Previously, we talked about the three buckets in our lives: work, home, and personal. Creating boundaries allows you to focus on each area within its own time so that each is treated as a priority in its dedicated space.

The time we spend doesn't need to be perfectly equal for each.

Sometimes we want to spend more time in one compartment than another. Remember, it's not about balance—balance doesn't exist—it's all about creating harmony.

So how can we focus in today's 24-7 culture? How can we possibly get to the deep work? The ability to focus seems like a luxury, but it's not—it's essential to purposeful productivity.

When we create strong borders around our time, we are able to become the best we can be. Think about it. When you are at work, you are a businessperson. When you are not, you play all the other roles: wife, mother, best friend, aunt, neighbor. Give each role in your life the opportunity to shine. Boundaries allow you to do that.

1. Do you feel like you've created strong boundaries for yourself?
2. Thinking through a typical day, are there places where you could set better boundaries?

Day 26
COMMUNICATION IS KEY

We often get frustrated when we find that people have invaded our boundaries. They expect emails at eight o'clock at night or calls on the weekend, but often it's because we have not clearly set our borders. Set boundaries with work and family—and make sure you clearly communicate them.

Let your work team know that you won't be responding to email immediately when it's outside of work hours. Many of us do feel the need to check in after hours, and that's okay. We just don't need to be at the beck and call of our business at every hour of the day. We can set aside a block of time to intentionally check in with work after hours; just make sure you don't leave that block open-ended. Set a start time *and an end time* for you to jump back into that work compartment.

I know this might feel difficult to do, especially if you don't work at a traditional office. Maybe you work from home or run your own business, so people think that you don't have set hours—this is when it's even more important to set up these compartments and clearly define them. Yes, it may take a few gentle reminders, but I promise you, they will get the message.

Your kids can also be taught to allow you to focus. Listen, if people can train a monkey to ride a tricycle, then your kids can be trained too. I taught my kids at a young age the sound of my work ringtone, and when they heard it they knew that was their cue to quiet down and allow me to talk on the phone. When I tell people this, they seem amazed that a four-year-old could do it, but have you ever seen preschoolers during a fire drill? They line up quietly and follow directions.

Do preschoolers know to do this right away? Absolutely not—they've been trained. As a former teacher, I just use the tricks I learned in the classroom—like doing pretend practice runs, acting out different scenarios, and giving my kids options and choices so they feel empowered to know what to do while I'm on my call. I made training fun, so my kids thought we were playing a game, but they were learning.

I found ways to make boundaries work, and you can, too, but you have to communicate.

1. How clearly have you communicated your boundaries? How well do people respect your boundaries?
2. What ideas do you have for better communicating your boundaries or training others to respect your boundaries?

EFFICIENT OR EFFECTIVE?

We need to change the way we think about being productive. We believe that we need to be efficient, to try to get as many tasks done in as little time as possible. We cram our day full with one task after the other in a mad dash to win the day.

Are we stopping to ask ourselves, though, if those tasks need to be done at all? Are those things we are hurrying to do really important? Or are we just mindlessly rushing through our to-do list, pinballing from one item to the next, exhausting ourselves? This is why we slip into bed and feel as though we didn't do enough or get enough done, that we weren't good enough even when we skipped lunch and did five tasks at the same time. Enough.

We are so busy working to be efficient that we don't have the time to catch our breath and ask ourselves the most important question of all: Why? Why are these tasks on our list? Why do they need to be done? Why are we killing ourselves to do it all?

Productivity isn't about being efficient—it's not about filling our day with tasks to quickly check off. It's about being *effective* and asking yourself if those tasks need to be done at all. I want to remind you: Productivity is not getting more done—it's focusing on what matters most.

Dishwashers are efficient; refrigerators are efficient. They are working hard with the least amount of resources and effort. And that is possible because they are machines—machines designed to do one thing over and over again: Dishwashers clean plates, and refrigerators keep things cool.

Unfortunately, when people focus on being efficient, the resource we target is time. We fail to realize that *being efficient is about getting things done; being effective is getting what's important done.* There's a big difference.

Efficiency is doing a lot of work; effectiveness is doing the *important* work. Quality wins every time. Yes, we want to use less energy and time, but not at the expense of quality.

1. Quality or quickness. Effectiveness or efficiency. Which one tends to be your go-to? What's usually your reasoning behind that approach?

2. What tasks are you efficiently doing? Can you take things slower and remind yourself to use your time effectively, so you focus on quality, not quantity?

THE MYTH OF MULTITASKING

We take a lot of pride in our multitasking ability. We mention it casually in job interviews, dropping it in the conversation like a beautiful shiny star. We mention it because it's a badge of honor, evidence of our ninja-like productivity prowess.

I used to feel that way, too, until I took the time to understand *why* multitasking was actually working against me.

Switching quickly from one task to the next is causing our brains to work harder than necessary, and this cognitive cost adds up. *Scientists have discovered that when we multitask, our productivity actually decreases by as much as 40 percent.* Yes, decreases. That's about sixteen hours we lose every week when we multitask.[5]

Why do we feel obligated to multitask? We think it makes us faster, but we now know from this study I just shared that not only is multitasking taking us longer, but it's also causing the quality of our work to suffer. We are doing our work half as well and taking twice as long—all while stressing ourselves out. That doesn't seem effective, does it?

When I posed this question to my community, one woman admitted:

If I am being honest, I think I multitask and get things done for a few reasons. I am very committed to seeing things through. . . . I don't want people to question my work, so maybe part of it is a need to prove I can do it all (and well) . . . proving my worth. Also, if I am focusing on "all the things," I don't have to dig deeper and get to the messy, vulnerable stuff.

I love the honesty she shared. I want to ask you if you think this is true for you. Do you pile more onto yourself, stressing yourself out, because you feel you have to prove your worth? Is it to keep yourself busy?

We want people to think we are good enough—that we deserve the praise, the job, all the good. Why do we feel the need to prove it?

1. Do you consider yourself a multitasker? Do you think you pile more on yourself because you feel you have to prove to yourself (or someone else) that you can do it all?
2. Have you noticed the quality of your work and/or relationships suffering when you've multitasked?

ARE YOU IN RHYTHM?

One common technique we use in an effort to be more productive with our time is to muscle through projects even when we feel tired or sluggish. We are so busy racing the clock that we don't realize our brains need time to rest.

The entire universe is dictated by rhythms: the rising and setting of the sun, the ebb and flow of the tides, the movement between seasons. All organisms, including humans, follow rhythms whether we realize it or not.

You've probably heard of your circadian rhythm, which is the 24-hour internal clock all living beings use to regulate eating and sleeping. That's what tells us to be awake for 16 hours and then asleep for 8 hours. Within the circadian rhythm, though, lives our ultradian rhythm, a shorter biological cycle of 90 to 120 minutes that repeats throughout the day.

During the first part of the ultradian rhythm, our alertness and brain-wave activity increase, making us feel energized and focused. After about 90 minutes, though, our brains begin to crave rest and renewal. Our brain requires about 20 minutes between each cycle to recover. In other words, the time we use to unplug is a key part of our day—not a frivolous break. We need to understand that periods of rest are not a reward for great work but are a requirement for great work to happen.

As Zen priest and Buddhist teacher Joan Halifax has shared, "There is the in-breath and there is the out-breath, and it's easy to believe that we must exhale all the time without ever inhaling. But the inhale is absolutely essential if you want to continue to exhale."[6]

We cannot work solidly for long blocks of time—our bodies simply don't work that way. And if we are insisting on blocking off a solid three- or four-hour power session, we really aren't doing more work; we are just wearing our brains out.

Stanford researchers discovered that your productivity actually drops dramatically once you hit the 50-hour mark in your workweek. Workers who put in 70 hours produce nothing more with those extra 20 hours. They are simply spinning their wheels, working longer but accomplishing less.[7] Again, it's not about the time you put in; it's the quality of that time.

Even people who love to work (and I count myself among them) are not performing at high levels once they get to a certain point. Once we understand and begin to work within our natural rhythms, we'll find we work more effectively, creating higher quality with less effort.

1. Try focusing on a task today uninterrupted for 90 minutes, then take a break for at least 15 minutes. What difference did this make for you in your energy level? Your focus? Your productivity?

2. Are there certain times of day when you feel work is easier? Do you think you are working within your ultradian rhythm?

Day 30
PAPER WORK(S!)

Most people believe that technology is necessary to do everything better, but it's simply not true. Technology is faster and sleeker, but it may surprise you to learn that writing down your ideas and plans on paper is more effective.

Bear with me as we don our lab coats for a minute and take a look at how our brains work. When we pick up a pen, our brain reacts differently than when we are tapping away on a keyboard. Writing triggers the reticular activating system (RAS), which signals our brain to pay attention.[8]

As I've mentioned, our brains are constantly bombarded with data. Our RAS is the filter that evaluates what information comes through. It's what wakes us up in the middle of a deep sleep when our babies cry or allows us to hear our own name in a crowded room. It tells our brains where to focus.

Writing triggers your RAS to tell the brain to stay alert—the information is important and needs to be saved where it can be accessed in the future. Typing, on the other hand, does not engage your RAS, so notes and plans tapped into a keyboard are more easily forgotten.

A joint study between Princeton and UCLA discovered that people who took notes with pens performed twice as well on tests as those using laptops. Knowing the laptop users had taken twice as many notes as those who had taken notes by hand, researchers had assumed computer users would be the clear victors. Taking notes on a computer *is* much more efficient, but it's not as effective. And that's the difference.

Don't get me wrong. Technology does need to play a key role in our days. I know it does in mine—even though I'm an advocate of paper planning. But we often feel obligated to use technology for *all* of our work. Unplugging, however, can really help our brains see problems in a different light.

Not only does paper engage your brain differently, but because it is more open-ended and flexible, it allows you to reframe thoughts and mold ideas in a way that ingrains the information.

Writing on paper deepens the relationship between the information and your brain. It allows you to see the bigger picture and uncover what's important, which is where you really want to spend your time.

1. When was the last time you put your plans on paper?
2. Here's your chance to put a plan to paper. Make a list below about something you need to accomplish. Did you find that you thought about the list differently than when you type it on a computer or on your phone?

Day 31

WHERE SHOULD I SPEND MY TIME?

Effectiveness comes down to priorities. Instead of focusing on trying to do everything, which leaves you feeling like you are herding cats, laser in on the important. The Pareto Principle will help you do that.

This centuries-old principle states that 20 percent of our efforts produce 80 percent of our results. This is not just a theory; the Pareto Principle has been proven again and again to hold true in all areas of life. You've probably heard it called the 80/20 rule:

20 percent of a meeting gives you 80 percent of the information.

20 percent of your wardrobe is what you wear 80 percent of the time.

20 percent of the people on your team do 80 percent of the work.

In other words, all things are not equal and therefore should not be treated as equal.

The ratio isn't perfect—it's not always right on the money at a perfect 80/20 split. Warren Buffett attributes 90 percent of his wealth to ten of the companies he invested in. Again and again, though, it's been proven that when you focus on less, you actually achieve more. *It's focused time that creates the greatest impact.* It's not doing more—it's doing what's most important. (Sound familiar?)

If it's been proven that the majority of our success will come from the minority of our tasks, why are we trying to do everything? Shouldn't we be giving the important tasks the larger portion of our time? If we focus on the top 20 percent of our customers and clients, we'll see our sales rise. That's not to say we ignore the other 80 percent, but the top 20 should be getting the lion's share of our attention, not the irritable client who definitely doesn't account for 80 percent of our business but wants an hour-long phone call every other day, or the projects that drag out endlessly with no finish line in sight. We have to limit the time we give these items so we can focus on the truly important.

1. Do you notice the Pareto Principle (the 80/20 rule) in your life and work?

   20% of my wardrobe is what I wear 80% of the time.
   TRUE   FALSE

   20% of my meetings give me 80% of the information I need.
   TRUE   FALSE

   20% of the people on my team do 80% of the work.
   TRUE   FALSE

2. What are some other places in your life where you can apply the Pareto Principle?

3. As you look at your task list, what falls into the unnecessary 80 percent?

Day 32

BUT WHAT WILL OTHERS THINK?

We get caught up in trying to do it all because we are trying to be perfect—to live the perfect life—to avoid the judgment of others. I think the hardest part about perfectionism is often the external pressure; there's so much perceived pressure from others to do things exactly right. We push ourselves to not make any mistakes because perfectionism is rooted in the fear of failure.

So, we lean into our stories, our beliefs, making sure "we always" or "we never." We set impossibly high standards for ourselves, and when we don't reach those standards, we relentlessly criticize ourselves for failing.

We make light of it, though. We coyly say we're a bit of a perfectionist when asked about flaws in a job interview, or we laugh and say we just have a certain way we want things done—our way. But perfectionism in our lives can be debilitating.

Too often our work and our environment push us to this notion of "good perfectionism"—an oxymoron that is confused with striving for excellence or setting high personal standards (both of which are entirely different from perfectionism).

Perfectionism keeps us from being effective and pushes us to be efficient if for nothing more than appearances. Many experts believe that most people who suffer from perfectionistic tendencies are not born that way—in many cases we are trained by others' expectations and stories so that we take perfection onto ourselves to help protect us from failure. We don't realize that without failure we wouldn't be as successful as we are. Our shortcomings and mistakes are all part of our path.

The good news is, if perfectionism is more of a mindset, then we can adjust our expectations. We can begin to realize when we are in that headspace and redirect. We can adjust our way of thinking about what it means to be good enough. We can focus on what is truly important without the weight of others' judgment resting heavily on our shoulders.

Don't take others' burdens onto yourself. We seem to want to throw that weight on our backs, but doing so only slows our pace. We have to walk away from this idea of focusing on everyone else's happiness at the expense of our own. When we let go of the pressure of this Pinterest-crazed world, we allow ourselves the freedom to move forward onto the path our North Star is guiding us toward.

1. Do you think you get caught up in perfectionism?

2. IF YOU CARED LESS ABOUT WHAT OTHER PEOPLE THOUGHT, DO YOU THINK YOU COULD BE HAPPIER?	WHY?
⬡ YES ⬡ NO	

THE DARK SIDE OF
THE TO-DO LIST

We rush through our days, and more often than not we find ourselves with a to-do list that stretches about five miles long. We feel pride in that fat line crossing out a task, proving that we are qualified to wear our badge of busy.

Our worth is not tied to the length of our to-do list. Yes, it makes us feel busy, but it doesn't make us productive—this is the dark side of the to-do list.

To-do lists tend to be unorganized and long because there's no filtering system. We simply add items as we think of them. When we scan our jumbled lists looking for our next task, our brains push us to choose the easiest wins—searching for a faster dopamine payoff (the chemical in our brains that's responsible for the feeling of satisfaction we receive when we accomplish something). You see, dopamine doesn't distinguish between important and unimportant; it just knows that crossing items off our lists feels good. And that means that the important tasks on our lists end up waiting to get crossed off. Let's be honest, it's usually those longer tasks that will move us toward the life we want. Our true priorities continue to get pushed farther and farther down on our lists, forgotten and undone.

A survey conducted by LinkedIn found that by the end of the average workday, only 11 percent of professionals had accomplished all the tasks on their list.[9] Our to-do lists are *supposed* to be a snapshot of our day, but here's the question: If 89 percent of professionals feel they've not accomplished their tasks, how do they feel at the end of the day?

To-do lists take energy away from the important tasks—the ones we must accomplish to create the impact we *really* want. We need to curate a list that highlights the route our North Star is guiding us toward, where each day we use our energy to get closer to our purpose and the big dreams and goals that go along with our North Star. We want a priority list. A priority list helps us look at the limited time we have so that we can choose where to spend our precious energy.

1. Thinking about how you spend your energy, rate your normal to-do list, with 1 being "Putting Out Fires" and 10 being "Tackling Important Priorities."

PUTTING OUT FIRES ☆ ☆ ☆ ☆ ☆ ☆ ☆ ☆ ☆ ☆ MY IMPORTANT PRIORITIES

2. Look at a to-do list you recently created. How many of those items were easy wins for a dopamine reward, and how many progressed you toward your dreams and goals?

YOU NEED A PRIORITY LIST

When we use a priority list, we stop wasting energy deciding what to do next, or whether to start with the hardest or the easiest tasks—instead, we work by priority. Focusing on our priorities is what separates the busy from the truly productive.

A good priority list takes the same amount of time to create as a to-do list, but because you filter it through your priority levels, you consciously choose where to spend your energy—and where you don't. The list is structured for you to begin your day at the top with the highest-priority tasks and work your way down. The feeling of overwhelm vanishes because you understand exactly where to start and what tasks you want to focus on next. You have a clear path for your day.

Our priority list is made of three levels: Escalate, Cultivate, and Accommodate. Let's look at each one. The first is *Escalate: Important and Urgent*. These tasks are pushing us toward long-term goals, *and* they have a pressing deadline. For example, last-minute adjustments to a project after receiving feedback from your boss, your car breaking down, or a report or term paper with an imminent deadline.

This section goes at the top of our list because this is where we want to start our day. These items are our top priority—we need to escalate them. However, we don't want to spend *all* of our time on Escalated Tasks because, by being in urgency mode, we don't allow ourselves the time to innovate or explore creative solutions. It's a defensive position, and we can't do our best work when we are reactive.

We can actually eliminate many of our Escalated tasks by planning ahead. Long-term projects can be scheduled out so they're finished with plenty of time left (thus doing a better job *and* making them not urgent); the car can be taken in for regular maintenance, so it does not break down; and so on.

We want to avoid Escalated situations whenever possible, but we'll never be able to eliminate them. Fires will always crop up— the boss assigns a last-minute presentation, the internet goes down, your kid gets sick at school—but for things that *are* in our control, we want to stay out of urgency mode.

1. What Escalated items are on your priority list this week?
2. Which ones could have been eliminated by planning ahead?

Day 35

TOSS YOUR TO-DO LIST

The second level of our priority list is *Cultivate: Important but Not Urgent.* These are activities that move us closer to our end goals because they are focused on future planning and self-improvement *but* have no looming deadline. Examples: creating a budget plan, long-term projects, or developing processes and workflows.

Being in a situation without an urgent deadline allows us to do our best work because we have the time to dive deeper into creative solutions; we are not in panic mode where we cannot think clearly. Because there's no urgency, though, we tend to push these items to the back burner until they finally do ignite, and then we end up feeling like we are fighting a wildfire with a garden hose.

While our priority list is divided into three sections, *we need to place the most emphasis on this section.* This is the area where we will grow by leaps and bounds. The seeds we plant today we will cultivate, and they will grow fruit for the future.

The final section of our priority list is *Accommodate: Unimportant but Urgent.* These are tasks with a pressing deadline, but they don't really help us focus on our North Star or our long-term goals. A few examples: the majority of the emails we receive or volunteering for a project that does not align with our priorities. We want to spend as little time in this section as possible, but because of the urgency, these tasks tend to scream out louder than the rest. We simply need to accommodate these tasks, not revolve our day around them.

It's a mindset shift of bumping these screaming tasks to the bottom of the list, to be completed after we've done our important work. That may cause some discomfort, but we need some disruption in order to change what we've always done.

I would like to challenge you to think about what tasks you can get rid of completely in this section by either deleting or delegating them: Do you have to load the dishwasher yourself, or can the other members of the household do that? Do you have to pick up the phone every time you get a call in the middle of your work time, or can you set a boundary for when you have the time to devote to talking? This is where you need to comb through your tasks and figure out how you want to focus your energy.

1. Which tasks from your to-do list belong in the Cultivate level of your priority list? Of these, which ones are you most excited about?

2. Which tasks at the Accommodate level can be deleted entirely or delegated? Challenge yourself so that you're expending as little energy as possible on these tasks.

GETTING CLEAR ON
WHAT'S IMPORTANT

Jeanne was a student in one of my courses who was just weeks away from returning to work after maternity leave. She seemed to love her newfound motherhood, and she loved her job, so she wanted to make sure she was giving work and home her true focus.

As any new mother will tell you, this is a challenge—there's so much to do, and adjusting to the new parenthood role takes some time. I got some good insight into Jeanne's struggles when she shared one of her completed exercises with me. The lesson was focused on looking at a list of tasks and deciding what on the list is important and what is merely urgent.

Jeanne had listed every single item as important. Every single one. No wonder she felt overwhelmed. Caring for a new baby is hard enough, but when you don't know your top priority, it's extraordinarily difficult to know where to start—which is when overwhelm sets in.

Not understanding what is important causes us to have priority blindness. We are so bombarded with tasks and requests that they blind us, and we lose sight of what is truly important. We pile more and more priorities on ourselves, which does nothing but weigh us down, keeping us from the life we want.

To make the process easier, I've created the CLEAR framework to help you differentiate the important from the merely urgent:

C Connected (Is this task connected to my North Star?)
L Linked (Is it linked to a goal?)
E Essential (Is it something that can only be done by me?)
A Advantageous (Will I see a good return on my investment?)
R Reality-Based (Does this task really need to happen, or is it tied to a story I'm telling myself?)

The process of "getting CLEAR" is easy: just use what I call the five-finger test. Ask yourself the five questions in the CLEAR framework, and each time you answer yes, simply raise a finger. If you have three or more fingers raised, you know the item deserves to be treated as important. Two fingers or fewer? That's an unimportant task.

1. Which of the five CLEAR framework elements is the easiest for you to discern most of the time in your decision-making? Which one is usually the hardest?

2. Have you ever felt like Jeanne where you found yourself overwhelmed and having trouble deciding what's important? How did you handle it?

SIMPLE SYSTEMS

I'm a terrible runner. Sometimes I see people running along the road, blissfully moving like graceful antelopes, and I so desperately want that. I go and lace up my shoes, I spend fifteen minutes stretching, and I run like an antelope. Until ten minutes later—when I remember how much I truly don't like running. I'm red-faced, out of breath, and officially spent. No gas left in the tank and no real desire to keep running.

You see, I'm in love with the *idea* of running—not the running itself. And I believe that's how people feel when they see highly disciplined ways of living. We see an image on Pinterest of a pantry where the food is divided into twenty-five thousand labeled containers (which are, of course, color coordinated!), or a book telling us that we need to fold our clothes in a very strict, very precise way.

We gather all the supplies, and we fold our clothes military style for fifteen minutes—until reality sets in. And then we are spent. No gas left in the tank and no real desire to use a ten-step process to fold a shirt.

Yes, the images are Pinterest-worthy, but is that really the life you want to live? I'll be honest, being a highly disciplined person sounds terrible—all that time *not* doing what you really want to do? You are setting yourself up for a future with some serious marble jar moments.

That's for the birds, my friend. Because here's the truth: It's not discipline you need—it's simple systems. Good, healthy systems aligned with the priorities you've discovered in this book. And the best news? Good systems run on autopilot once we establish them.

Systems are a key part of living the life we want, because while it's important to spend time focused on priorities, we still have all the other tasks to do. There are the not-so-glamorous activities like home maintenance, managing finances, getting dinner on the table, and laundry. What is it about laundry? How is it possible that we need a mountain's worth of clothes cleaned every single week? But we do. I hear women asking, begging, to know if there's a magic solution to keep everything running and still make time for what's important—and there is. Systems. Strong systems harness the patterns of habits and make tasks happen automatically. Like I said—magic.

1. How do you feel when you see highly disciplined people? Are you happy with how your life runs?
2. On a scale of 1 (utter disorganization) to 10 (everything is running along great), how would you rate your current household systems? What prompted your rating?

PLAY TO YOUR STRENGTHS
AND YOUR WEAKNESSES

Here's the catch: Systems need to work for you. They should be tightly bound to the life we *really* want to live; they should play to our strengths and our weaknesses to make life feel easier.

I'm guessing that you are more like me. I've got enough on my plate worrying about whether I'm raising responsible kids, whether I'm accomplishing my goals, and whether my work feels strong than to worry about the Pinterest-worthy lifestyle.

We need to create systems that feel attainable and fit the lifestyle we really want—not the one we think we are *supposed* to want.

When I was growing up, we always had a set of color-coordinated towels perfectly placed on the towel bar in each bathroom. I remember asking my mother, "Why did we have such fancy, fluffy towels in our bathrooms that no one was allowed to use?"

I recall her shrugging her shoulders as she meticulously refolded and straightened the towels on the bar and explained, "That's just what you are supposed to do."

Our job isn't to question why; it's to live up to the expectations.

It wasn't her fault. She was following the rules—the story she told herself: *Ladies with nice houses have beautifully useless linens.*

I think that's the moment I decided I would never have a towel bar in my bathroom. And I don't. Every time I move into a house, I take down the towel bars and put in a set of hooks. In my heart of hearts, I'm honest with myself. I know I won't trifold a towel and position it beautifully on the bar. Quite frankly, no one else in my house will either. But we will place it on a hook.

It's the same with clothes. I am not good at folding clothes, and I don't enjoy it. There are about ten thousand things I'd rather do than fold clothes, including hanging by my fingernails.

Recognizing my weakness, I set up closets so more clothes can be hung. Very few items go into drawers, and those that do have bins to create sections that allow me to toss in items like socks and underwear while keeping everything organized. I don't want to spend my life folding. I want to spend it living.

Systems should bring harmony to your life, but when they aren't in tune they can feel disruptive. This might be why we've all started and quit a thousand different ways to keep ourselves organized, resulting in us feeling like failures. But it was the system that failed—not us. The system simply didn't work for the way *we* work.

Play to your strengths *and* your weaknesses. Let's embrace our imperfectly beautiful selves and then make our systems work to our advantage.

1. When it comes to doing things around the house, what are your strengths? Your weaknesses?
2. As you look back on some of the systems you have tried to establish that didn't work, what about them didn't work for you?

Day 39

EVER FEEL BRAIN DEAD?

Your brain takes up a mere two percent of your body mass but consumes an astonishing twenty percent of your calories each day.[10] Your brain is a calorie-burning machine, so it loves to conserve energy when it can. Then it can apply big effort to the important items you want to tackle, like your goals.

Your brain, just like your body, has a limited amount of calories, and when your brain is working hard making decisions, decision fatigue sets in.

That moment at the end of the day when you feel brain-dead? That feeling is real—your brain is literally running out of calories and just can't function. It's not about willpower or discipline. Your brain simply has no gas left in the tank and no real desire to keep making good choices.

Most times we aren't even aware we are low on mental energy. Our brain continues working but starts to look for shortcuts. It does this in two different ways:

Acts Impulsively: In other words, it stops spending the energy needed to think through your actions. *I'm hungry*

*and the donut that's been sitting out in the break room since
yesterday looks good. I should eat it.*

Does Nothing: We simply choose not to choose. *I know my
budget is tight, but I can't decide which of these pairs of
shoes looks better. I'll get both.*

Our perfectly rational brain loses its ability to make good
decisions when we overload it with work. Understanding decision
fatigue felt like a lightbulb moment for Holly. As a former army
officer, she was used to making fast-paced decisions in her job.
Being retired means that many of her decisions may seem less significant, but in her own words, "Since they involve my family, they
are at the top of my 'Get it right the first time' list. . . . I don't want
to keep space in my mind for 'What do I have to do next?' Let's
just write it down and make it a scheduled item. Less stress, less
worry—I know I've got it handled."

Holly is taking charge and taking the thinking out of it. That's
what we need to do too. We want to get our brains working at full
capacity by allowing them to focus on what's most important—not
on trivial decisions.

Using habits to our advantage does that. Tying habits into our
systems allows us to streamline our thinking and helps eliminate
decision fatigue so we can spend our energy in the most impact-
ful way.

1. How often would you say you experience that brain-dead feeling due to decision fatigue?

2. Which shortcuts does your tired brain seem to prefer? Now that you're aware of it, do you recognize any other personal "symptoms" of decision fatigue?

TAKING THE THINKING OUT OF IT

We hear about *habits*, and we think about biting our nails or snacking too much or smoking. We think all habits are bad, but researchers at Duke University found that about 40 to 45 percent of the actions we take each day are actually habits, not really decisions.[11]

That's a good thing! How taxing would it be if we had to think about every little action we make throughout our day? What would it be like if we had to concentrate every morning on getting dressed? When we first learned to put on our pants as toddlers, it took immense effort. We now get dressed without giving it a second thought—we can have a conversation or watch TV while doing it. Here's what's really interesting: Each time you put on your pants, you put the same leg in first. Yes, every time. You see, putting on pants is a habit.

Using habits allows your brain to focus its energy on what really matters in your day. Charles Duhigg, author of *The Power of Habit*, shared that when you start implementing habits, "the brain starts working less and less. The brain can almost completely shut down. . . . And this is a real advantage, because it means you have all of this mental activity you can devote to something else."[12] Something else, you know, like your priorities and goals. Habits free up our mental space so we can focus.

People who appear to be disciplined are really people who have harnessed the power of habits. This is what makes them seem disciplined when in reality a never-ending supply of willpower doesn't exist.

We need to leverage our habits to free up our brain space to make the choices that really matter. Building strong habits isn't hard; it just takes some extra energy at the beginning. Once they are established, habits require less effort, less energy, and less thinking to maintain. They take the thinking out of tasks. Your brain stops wasting calories and channels all its energy to move you forward.

1. Think about your morning routine—a routine is simply habits with one following the next. Do you enjoy your morning routine? What would you like to change?

2. Name three small decisions you make each day that would simplify your life if you made them habits that you no longer think about it.

CREATE GOOD HABITS

The way to create good habits is to *identify the cues*. Charles Duhigg defines these as the trigger to tell our brain to instigate the habit.[13] Cues can be as simple as leaving our gym shoes by the door to help trigger us to run after work, or leaving our planners on our desks to remind us to start each day by creating a priority list. Cues are the biggest key to unlocking our habits because once we know what triggers an action, we can begin to *define the behavior*.

Forming a habit does take intention, so it's important to make sure not to skip the final step—*make a plan*. A good plan includes the three Rs—*record, reward,* and *redirect*. We want to track our progress. When we are working on cultivating daily habits, it's difficult for us to see our progress unless we find a way to track growth. *What gets written gets measured; what gets measured gets achieved.* We want to be mindful with establishing these habits, so it's important to stop and take note. A simple habit tracker is ideal in helping you track and measure your progress.

Another important part of creating a plan is to make sure you reward yourself. Small rewards work as celebrations and springboards to keep you moving. Brain research shows that rewards are a key part of setting the patterns of habits in place. We require positive reinforcement at the beginning to act as a message to the brain, telling it this is an activity worth remembering in the future.

Let me share some unfiltered honesty with you: We will stumble. We will stray off track. It happens to all of us. We need to remind ourselves that habits take time and there may be days when we forget our cues or feel frustrated. We can't get caught up when we fail; we need to be prepared to pick ourselves back up, recover, and redirect.

1. For the positive habits you're wanting to establish, what are the cues that will help trigger the process each day?
2. How can you reward yourself for staying on track? The reward can be small—even as simple as giving yourself a kind word or listening to a favorite song.

Day 42

BREAKING BAD HABITS

I've walked with you through the process of establishing a habit—but what about habits we don't really love? Let me share how I used this same process to my own advantage to break a bad habit.

I am terrible about checking email. Terrible in the sense that I'm like Pavlov's dog. Every time I hear the little ping of a new email, I must immediately stop what I'm doing and go check it. The need for the little hit of dopamine mixed with my perfectionism addiction drives me to constantly strive to zero out my inbox count. When I hear that ping I begin to feel the itch calling to me to stop whatever I'm doing to go check it. It doesn't seem to matter that at least 25 percent of the time it's spam. In my mind, it must be checked immediately.

My first step was acknowledging that I had accidentally built up a habit of checking email incessantly. I knew I wanted to limit my email time so I could reclaim my time for my important work— that was my *why*.

I channeled my inner Nancy Drew and discovered a few cues that caused me to be in my inbox far too much: the ping of the computer when a new email arrived and the inbox email count at the bottom of my screen. I needed to kill the cues and redefine my behavior. I set a goal to establish a new habit of checking email four times a day: in the morning, before lunch, midafternoon, and early evening. I set a reminder on my phone to notify me when it was time to dive into my inbox.

I'll be honest: Thinking of checking only four times a day almost gave me the shakes because I have a couple of excuses I tell myself, like *Other people rely on me to reply quickly!* and *I can't help myself!* I acknowledged that these were excuses. Then I made my plan. Other than my four check-in times, my email program would have to be closed out to eliminate the temptation, and any noisy notifications were turned off on my phone. I even turned off the vibrate option.

I figured I was spending at least an extra thirty minutes of my day mindlessly checking email, so to reward myself, I gifted those thirty minutes back. I set myself up with a habit tracker to keep up with my progress, and on the days I did well, I used my thirty bonus minutes to do whatever I wanted. I read fiction books, took baths, painted my nails—all things I told myself I didn't have time to do before. It took time, but I now feel more in control of my email—it no longer controls me. And that's a good feeling.

That's the feeling I want to permeate our days. With systems in place we have less stress, we are more effective, and nothing falls through the cracks. When we create systems playing to our strengths and weaknesses, we have gas in our tanks and real desire for the life we are living.

1. It's your turn: Acknowledge a bad habit you want to break. What's your *why*? Then work through the process from there.
2. How will you reward yourself for breaking this habit? If possible, can you come up with a quick daily reward?

MAKE IT AUTOMATIC

This idea of "taking the thinking out of it" can be applied to all kinds of tasks, from our routines to our household chores. Remember, we want to be effective. We want to take care of our work, so tasks never have a chance to ignite into urgency, but we also want them to happen with as little effort as possible.

Automations are systems for things you don't do every day but need to get done. The word *automation* may sound like technical jargon, but it's not tech at all. It's simply a task that happens automatically, without too much thinking. We set up automations because these tasks we do on an irregular basis tend to fall between the cracks, like pennies between our couch cushions. *When we don't have these tasks scheduled somewhere, they end up getting scheduled nowhere.*

Chores are a fabulous task to automate because, let's be honest, who wants to think about chores? No one. But it does us no good to bring home the bacon and fry it up in a pan if the kitchen is burning down around us. We have to keep life moving—even the not-so-glamorous parts.

Automations work in thousands of places at home and at the office: website maintenance, grocery shopping, ordering office supplies, dusting, laundry. We can even use automations to break down tasks that need to be done throughout the year.

I create a big master list for myself for those tasks and chores. Then at the start of each month, I simply plug these tasks into my calendar. For example, we deep clean the fridge in January, April, July, and October; we start looking for summer camps in January. As you can see, some tasks happen once, and other tasks happen multiple times a year.

Automations can take our big, overwhelming projects and tasks and make them manageable. Taxes are a great example—we all know taxes are due in April, so why do we wait until the last minute to pull together everything we need?

Break the task down and make it easier. In January create a folder with a checklist for the paperwork you are expecting to trickle in over the next few months; in February organize your office area to help uncover any documents that may be helpful for filing; in March make your appointment with your CPA; and in April relax, because your nerves aren't shot from the stress. Set up automations so that each of these pieces of the puzzle is assigned a time and space.

Creating automations allows each task to happen with minimal effort. That's a system that simplifies life and allows it to run with less stress. It's truly being effective.

1. What weekly, monthly, or annual task would you love to automate so that it doesn't become a fire to put out, but doesn't fall through the cracks either?

2. As you decide which tasks to automate, don't forget to bring in others to play their parts. What could you delegate to your staff, your coworkers, or other family members?

Day 44

STOP HUSTLING

Hustle is one of those buzzwords people like to use, especially when it comes to business. In truth, *hustle isn't about business; it's about busyness. Hustle* is just a more aggressive word for *busy,* meaning "to jostle" and "to crowd and push roughly"[14]—and often what we crowd is our day. We jam-pack our schedule from start to finish with activities, tasks, projects, and errands. We don't give ourselves the space to breathe.

Despite what social media tells us, *life is not about the hustle.* But we have this learned helplessness that tells us we cannot own our day, that it does not truly belong to us. If this is true, who does our day belong to? Our bosses? Our families? Other people who push their agendas and priorities on us that we accept out of guilt?

Let's remind ourselves that we are in charge. Because when we feel in control of our schedule, we don't just survive; we thrive.

We need to be present in our lives, accountable for where our day takes us, and responsible for our choices. Without presence, productivity can become busyness, where we find ourselves performing task after task that have little meaning to us in the long run. When we can act upon our North Star on a daily basis, accomplishments will follow.

Being present simply requires filtering out the minutia, purposely choosing not to do everything, and instead intentionally planning our day. Creating structure for our days can be beautifully simple and takes only minimal effort—but the rewards are great. I've created a system that you can easily personalize and customize to you and your life called the 5 Ps of planning: Purge, Process, Prioritize, Protect, Propel.

A system like the 5 Ps helps make it easier to focus on what's important. Over the next few days, let's unpack this together and go through each of these steps.

1. Do you feel like you have been owning your days, or do you feel like they own you?

MY DAYS OWN ME ☆ ☆ ☆ ☆ ☆ ☆ ☆ ☆ ☆ I OWN MY DAYS!

2. Who in your life has been structuring the majority of your days in the past six months (intentionally or unintentionally)? List those people in order. Where would you place yourself on that list?

Day 45

GET IT OUT OF YOUR HEAD

When everything we need to accomplish is swirling around in our heads, it can take up a lot of space. Using our brains like giant filing cabinets for our tasks is simply not effective. Purging our task list from our heads creates the space we need. It's as easy as doing a brain dump, so we can move it out of our brains and onto some paper.

This first step—*purging*—allows you to take time to think through the entire week. I do a weekly purge on Sundays for my home and on Mondays for work. I purposely keep these planning sessions separate because I want to make sure that in my head, these two sections have their own boundaries and space.

Your weekly brain dump can take place on your own or with a team. Most of us know what planning alone looks like, so I'll share with you how I do this first step for home tasks with my family.

Every Sunday afternoon we have an automation called "team planning." The four of us sit around our kitchen table and brainstorm everything we need to do or accomplish over the next seven days: homework, chores, meals, sports practices, and so on. You can do this on a sheet of blank paper, but I have a notepad called the

Weekly Kickstart that is designed to help make this first step even easier. There's room for us to write down our brain dump list, and it has space to plug in any timed appointments (like dentist visits or carpool times). This then becomes our master list, which I post in a prominent place in our kitchen for everyone to reference.

Every one of us is responsible for making our team work. My family knows to check the Weekly Kickstart to see what needs to happen and when. They don't need to ask me, and I don't have to use up precious brainpower reminding them. (Even when my kids were little and couldn't read, we used this system. I would use stickers and drawings to convey tasks, and I set up a digital clock, so they always knew the time.)

This first step of planning doesn't have to feel too rigid or constraining—it can become a highlight of your week if you allow it.

1. When is the best time for you to complete the first step in the 5 Ps and do a weekly purge? Decide first if you want to do two purges: one for work and one for home, and then think about your schedule.

2. How do you think doing this weekly will help you have a little more brain space? Do you think it will help your team (at work or at home) be more accountable for themselves if you do this planning together?

Day 46

EVERY DAY IS A NEW
OPPORTUNITY

One of the biggest mistakes I see people make is planning out the entire week in one sitting, slotting in what they'll do Friday afternoon even though it's still six days away. They purge but don't take the time to follow up with step two: *process*.

We need to process each day as it comes, making a daily plan for the greatest impact. This is the secret to making our days achievable. Why? Because let's say Monday is a great start to the week. You feel good and have a productive day. But then Tuesday happens. Tuesday starts out with a child crawling into your bed at 3:00 A.M., followed by a morning with you downing allergy meds like Tic Tacs thanks to the pollen in the air. Your head feels like it's chockablock full of cotton, and you never seem to recover.

Unfortunately, if you've already planned every single day of your week, Wednesday opens with you feeling ten steps behind because you have to make up for that hot mess of a Tuesday. Before you know it, it's Thursday and it feels like you'll never get ahead.

We need to treat each day like a new opportunity. Some days will be amazing, and we'll get twice as much accomplished as we hoped, and some days, well, some days are just Tuesdays. And that's okay.

The purge we do at the start of the week gives us a bird's-eye view of what we want to accomplish, so we need to pull from this list to process what we want to accomplish each day. Ten minutes at the start of every day to focus solely on *that* day gives us the grace and flexibility we need for those "Tuesday mornings."

Break down the big tasks and choose what is most important to get done, and then focus only on those steps you can accomplish today. Think through your energy level, mood, and expectations, and then set your intention for that day only. *That's the biggest secret to setting ourselves up for success: making sure our days are actually achievable.*

We often set ourselves up for failure by putting far too much on our plates. We have to ask ourselves: *What can I accomplish today?* It's okay to start small and allow your capacity to grow. *Small steps are better than no steps.*

1. For me, processing is simply an extension of my morning routine. Every day, once I arrive at my office, I begin with ten minutes of focused processing time—before checking emails, before other people have the opportunity to fill my calendar with their priorities. When and where is going to be your best processing time?
2. How would it feel to "treat each day as a new opportunity" each morning?

Day 47

DECLUTTER YOUR DAY

I want you to start giving yourself permission to *prioritize* the work that will move you forward. This is the third of the five Ps of planning. If we are hyperfocused solely on results, we can lose sight of our North Star. Opportunities for growth and learning are often seen as an indulgence because they focus on the long-term benefits rather than immediate results, but this is the work that will ultimately drive us toward our ideal life. This is the important work we need to prioritize more.

We have to limit the amount of time we are giving unimportant items. And, yes, I used the term *giving* here very intentionally. We are gifting time to tasks and activities as if our time were infinite and we can generously hand it all away.

One of my favorite systems to help create space in my day is batching—intentionally collecting similar activities for an intentional block of time to maximize time, energy, and focus. This works even if we batch unimportant tasks because then these *distractions* are done at one time, allowing us to spend the majority of our time on our priorities. It helps declutter our days. Instead of doing the same tasks again and again, we streamline them and do them in fewer sessions, so they disrupt less of our day.

Once we group our activities together, we can set aside an amount of time to work on the batched tasks. I call this amount of time a container—it gives me boundaries and a structure from which I can work and tells me when I need to walk away. This is key, especially when batching unimportant tasks.

Batching works with the way our brains work: It moves with our ultradian rhythm, so it uses our energy effectively. It takes over twenty minutes for the brain to get into the zone of doing deeper work. Batching allows us to get into that elusive flow, a deeper state of thinking, so we get higher-quality work using less time.

1. You saw an example of me batching email when we talked about habits earlier in the book. What are some tasks you can batch together?
2. If you take a few minutes in the morning to prioritize your task list, how do you think you will feel at the end of the day?

FILL YOUR CALENDAR

Throughout this book I've been preaching to you about not filling your day, but now I'm going tell you just the opposite. I'm warning you because I don't want you to think I've lost it—just stick with me here and I'll explain. Ready?

I want you to fill your calendar. Fill it up in the morning during your process time, slot in your important tasks, schedule your batches, block your time. Use your ultradian rhythm as your guide to make sure you block off time for focus and time for breaks.

Why do we want to do this? Because we want to fill our calendars first. This is how we *protect* our planning. A wide-open calendar is an invitation for others to cram it full with their priorities and demands rather than our own. This helps us establish our boundaries and allows us to "burn the boats" just as Archimedes did.

Higher-ranking priorities should get the lion's share of your time, so block off those items first. These are nonnegotiable time blocks that belong to you, so treat them as you would an appointment with someone else—you wouldn't cancel a doctor's visit or arrive thirty minutes late. Right? This is an appointment with you and your goals.

Here's the catch: To time block effectively, we need to be careful not to line up our blocks one right after the other. We need to allow for some buffers so there's some breathing room—to allow for the expansion of ideas. Similar to when we drive our cars, we don't tailgate and ride the bumper of the car in front of us. We give ourselves a buffer to allow for sudden braking or swerves in the road.

Giving ourselves buffers provides us the flexibility we need to be proactive. The solution can be as easy as giving yourself a 50 percent buffer. If it takes you ten minutes to get to the soccer fields, leave the house fifteen minutes before you need to get there. You'll feel less stressed and flustered, and if you arrive early, you can take that time and spend it on something you like to do. I consider this a hidden pocket of time in which I have focused conversations with my kids. It's amazing the deep connections we can make when we strip away everything else.

Buffers give us the flexibility we need so our systems don't fail. When we create tight timelines for ourselves, the margin for success is razor thin. Let's set ourselves up for success by allowing ourselves the room we need.

1. What buffers have you already built into your day? Do you need to create some additional ones?
2. What could you do with those hidden pockets of time you will gain by adding buffers? (Think about fun activities like reading a book or calling a friend.)

A LITTLE WATER IN YOUR WELL

The last step in this system is what I consider one of the most important: *propel*. We need to give ourselves a little *velocity*—set up our dominoes.

When asked about finding inspiration Ernest Hemingway said, "As long as you can start, you are all right." He recommended that "the important thing is to have good water in the well."[15] Hemingway's idea of leaving water in the well means we never want to leave a task or a project without knowing how we will pick it back up. We want to return to our tasks with the same momentum.

When I'm writing books I plug in my computer before heading to bed, so it's fully charged when I get up. Stacked on top are my glasses and notes for what I need to do next. Knowing my computer is there waiting reduces the energy I need to start. It's a little domino that helps get my entire line of dominos moving in the morning.

We can use this idea in all areas of our day to help build momentum: leaving lunch items ready to assemble on the counter after cleaning up dinner, keeping backpacks by the back door where they won't be forgotten, placing a note in your planner with next-action items.

When it comes to leaving water in the well, one of my favorite methods is to create a dedicated folder for projects. You can create a project log to staple on the inside flap of the folder where you write out the date, time spent, and next steps. The benefit of this is not only the water in the well but also the breadcrumb trail of what you've accomplished. This helps you see how much time you spent on the project (which will help you with planning in the future), and you'll get a feeling of accomplishment for what you've done.

I think breadcrumbs are important because many of us under-value the amount of time we've spent—always thinking we haven't done enough or didn't work hard enough. It's hard, though, to argue with data. Breadcrumbs show you your success.

1. Propelling is an important part of creating structure and building momentum. What are some ways you can "leave water in your well" at the end of each day?
2. What three things can you do at the end of the day today to give you momentum for tomorrow?

Day 50

THE DAILY DOWNLOAD

The Daily Download will add significant water to your well. This five-minute activity is responsible for doubling my productivity, and I believe in it so strongly that I created a special notepad for it. The framework of it is simple; you can even use a sheet of paper if you'd like.

Minute one is spent reflecting on your accomplishments for the day. I find, at the end of the day, it's hard to think of all the good we've done, so taking one minute to reflect makes a huge difference. It's important to count the marbles in our jars.

Minute two is focused on evaluating your day. Did we put too much on our plate? How was our stress? Our attitude? Our focus? If you consistently score high on stress and low on attitude, you need to make some adjustments.

Minute three is for assessing what you did to move closer to accomplishing your goals. Check in and ask yourself each day to assess how you are inching closer to your North Star. A little progress each day makes a difference.

Minute four is all about gratitude. Find three things you are grateful for. The trick is it needs to be specific to that day. For example, "I am grateful for lunch with Susan because she helped me feel confident about my project." According to happiness expert Shawn Achor, if you do this for twenty-one days, you'll set a pattern of low-level optimism, even if you think you are naturally a pessimist.[16]

Minute five is for setting up your dominoes. Write down a few notes about tomorrow's action items—the important tasks you would like to focus on. You aren't planning tomorrow; you are simply giving yourself guidance on what to work on next, a little water in your well.

The Daily Download takes just five minutes to do, but it will dramatically change the way you feel about your days. I complete this quick activity at the end of each workday, so I close out the day on a high note. I leave the page sitting on my desk, so the added bonus is that when I go into my office the following morning, I start my day with a boost—that's the best kind of water to leave in your well.

1. Which of these five minutes comes the most naturally to you?
2. Which of the five minutes is a little more challenging? Why?

CREATE HARMONY
FOR YOURSELF

Harmony can be found in the 168 hours we have each week, but so many people choose to focus—almost hawklike—on just the 24 hours of each day. Twenty-four hours is such a tiny snapshot of the whole picture, literally one-seventh of our week. And yet each day is treated as if it stands alone, so there's a tendency to look at this tiny snapshot as our chance at achieving this mythical balance.

This means all our priorities—all the things that matter the most—have to squeeze in and find time during this small window. Time management expert Laura Vanderkam calls this the "24-Hour Trap" because it's simply not feasible. She shares, "Any given 24 hours might not be balanced, but the 168-hour week as a whole can be."[17] In other words, we have to stop looking at our lives as individual days and begin to look at the bigger picture.

When we zoom out and look at the week as a whole, we can begin to find harmony in unexpected places. We need to stop treating each day as its own scorecard to be checked for balance. Look at your week as a whole and see if maybe you are spending more time on your priorities than you realize. We tend to beat ourselves up and to notice only the things we didn't do well, when in reality we are doing much better than we think.

If we view the week as seven opportunities for success, we have a greater chance of achieving harmony. Let's talk about a common balance complaint: "I work too much and never seem to make it home for dinner with the family."

If you have a job that requires occasional late hours or you travel for work, making it home for dinner every single night will be difficult. By setting yourself up for this rigid expectation of seven nights a week, you are setting yourself up for failure.

If you choose, instead, to look at the harmony of 168 hours, you might notice that while you didn't make it home for dinnertime on Wednesday, you did spend time together on Sunday, Monday, Thursday, and even Friday. You were together four evenings out of seven. In the big picture? That's success!

1. How do you define a "successful" day? If you're being honest, is this definition achievable on a daily basis?
2. If you choose to look at the past week in terms of weekly wins rather than looking for balance every day, will you feel more satisfied?

REDEFINE SUCCESS

When it comes to harmony, why don't we zoom out even further? Let's get to the heart of why dinner with the family is a priority. For most people, it's not about the act of sitting down and eating at the end of the day that's important. It's the intentional time spent together that matters.

So, who says this has to happen around the dinner table? Could meaningful time happen in the morning? Is it possible to go into work a little bit later so you can have some time together before work happens? Or could you scoot away from the office and schedule in a lunch once a week with your family? What about weekends? If work keeps you burning the midnight oil during the workweek, can you schedule in some very intentional blocks of focused family time on the weekend?

The priority is enjoying time together as a family. We need to loosen up our narrow definition of how we spend time on our priorities. When we do that, harmony can flourish.

> *Need to do a lot of networking for your job? Who says it has to happen at happy hour? Why not try hosting some coffee meetups in the morning or midafternoon?*

Don't think you have time for date night with your spouse? Try meeting once or twice a month for lunch dates while the kids are in school. Maybe even throw in the occasional lunch at a hotel where you get sandwiches from room service and some "exercise."

No time for your favorite pastimes, such as reading? Carry your current read with you everywhere you go, and then grab those hidden pockets of time while standing in line at the grocery store or while waiting for piano lessons to be over. That's how Stephen King reads five hours every single day while still publishing bestselling fiction of his own.

My point is, there are a thousand ways we can redefine success when we get creative. We just have to treat our priorities as priorities.

1. What choices are you making that add stress to your life? What changes can you make to ensure that you treat your priorities as actual priorities?
2. Is there a priority that you constantly feel like you haven't done well prioritizing? How can you get creative so you can feel more successful?

Day 53

SLEEP LIKE A SHARK

I'm like a shark—I have to keep moving. If I stop, I die."

Those words were tossed out lightheartedly by a good friend of mine recently during a call. We were discussing all the never-ending tasks and events filling up our days. I laughed when she said it, but her phrase stuck with me.

We all feel busy—overbusy, if we're being honest—and we feel as if that's normal life. It seems like everyone is doing it all and, according to their camera roll, doing it well. And that's created a lot of sharks in the water—people who think that if they dare to stop moving, they will lose their importance—their place in the world.

Sharks glide through the salty water at the top of the food chain, but they are burdened with the constant task of movement. For sharks to breathe, oxygen-rich water must continually flow over their gills. If a shark stops moving, it will sink to the sandy bottom of the ocean floor and suffocate. *So, how do sharks sleep?*

It wasn't until a recent expedition to Guadalupe Island that the mystery was solved. Scientists were tracking a large great white shark named Emma. During the daylight hours she stayed deep in the warm waters, stalking her prey swimming above. But as night fell, Emma's behavior began to shift drastically. She settled her giant body near the sandy bottom of the shallow waters and placed herself directly into the oncoming current. With jaws gaping open, she appeared to go into a sleeplike state. The swift current passed effortlessly over her gills, keeping her alive while allowing her to slow down and conserve her energy.[18]

If the ocean's apex predator can learn to slow herself down to allow some time for rest, surely we can too. This is an animal that truly cannot stop moving, yet she's found a way to recharge. This downtime, this white space, is important for the shark to thrive. We need that too.

When we are busy, there's very little time for quiet; the noise begins to feel so natural, we don't even notice it. But this is the white space you want—strike that—it's the white space you *need* so you can dive deep into who you really are and who you want to be.

1. When was the last time you slowed down enough to all yourself some space and rest? How did you feel afterward?
2. Do you feel it's an expectation in today's society to fill our days and constantly be busy? How do you feel at the end of an especially busy day?

Day 54

ADULTS NEED RECESS TOO

To be truly productive we need to give our brains a little space to *play and explore*—some unstructured time.

But I get it. We feel like we can't disconnect—it's become an expectation to turn around emails and texts at all hours. Before smartphones, we clocked out on the weekends, and we could go on vacation without worrying whether our bosses were going to call. Smartphones are designed to connect us, but rather than pulling us closer to those we love, they are chaining us to our work. We have to choose to carve out space.

I know what you might be saying to yourself. *I don't have time to play.* But I would challenge you and tell you that we all have time for white space. We do. We have spaces of time in our schedule already—we just don't purposefully carve them out. And because we don't create this space with intention, we aren't reaping the full benefits of our white space. I'll show you what I mean:

Raise your hand if, in the last twelve months, you have binge-watched a TV show or taken a silly online quiz, maybe to find out which *Star Wars* character you are most like. If you chased away boredom by playing a mindless game on your phone, your hand should be up too. I'm betting we all have our hands raised (and, yes, mine included).

We have the time, but the idea of intentionally creating space for this unstructured time feels silly because we are grown-ups, and we don't think we need recess. But we do. White space is essential for our own well-being.

Recently we went on a five-day white-space vacation with my best friend's family—and absolutely no technology. Two families: four full-time working parents, two tween girls, two teenage boys, and zero devices. None. Crazy, right? You know what happened, though? Our kids sat up late and had deep conversations with one another, they collected grasshoppers in a Pringles can, they studied ants gathering together cracker crumbs for two hours. They laughed. They interacted.

For five glorious days we were all untethered from our computers, from our televisions, from our phones. During this white space, I realized we are often so focused on our screens we forget to look around. We forget to interact with the world around us—we don't look up; we walk, eyes down, hunched over our phones like addicts. We have lost the ability to truly connect. Connect with others *and* connect with ourselves.

We have to turn off the phone so we aren't tempted to peek at the screen, put our email on pause, and trust that our teams at work can carry on without us checking in on them again and again. That is a good thing.

1. What is your biggest hesitation about disconnecting for a while?
2. If you were to cut your social media time in half this week and plan to do something fun with at least a few of those hours, what activity would be at the top of your list? Write it down here:

(Now that you've admitted it, make it happen!)

Day 55

WHEN IS IT ENOUGH?

Kelly is a great mom who struggles with the many roles a single parent has to play. It's not easy being the sole provider and being in charge of everything at work and home. It's easy to forget to take time for yourself. Kelly shared in my community, "My boundaries for self-care always go by the wayside when I don't feel like I did enough to earn the time."

I don't think Kelly is alone in feeling this way, so I challenged her by asking, "When *do* you feel you've earned the time?" I was curious because for most people, the feeling of having done enough is like pouring water into a bucket with a hole in it—it's never filled.

Kelly decided to track her time and discovered that her problem wasn't whether she had done enough; it was whether she *appeared* to do enough. She realized she "was so focused on if other . . . people thought [she'd] put enough hours in at the office." It wasn't about her own expectations but her feeling that others didn't think she had a right to that time.

I know you are nodding your head with me here as we realize that this is yet another story we are telling ourselves. But the beauty of acknowledging our stories is that we have the ability to rewrite our own endings. A few weeks later, Kelly shared this win: "Woo Hoo! Today I sent the kids to play outside for 15 minutes after dinner while I sat down and read a book! For pleasure! I decided after completing an awesome meeting and taking care of my girls it was ENOUGH. I deserved it."

I think my favorite part is that last sentence: *I deserved it.* She does deserve it, and so do you, but often our inner critic tells us otherwise. It barks loudly at us, telling us we should be busy to be worthy. It's the voice that tells us anything we do for ourselves is selfish. But giving space to ourselves is self-care, and self-care isn't selfish.

1. Do you feel the need to be busy? How does it feel when you have some extra time to yourself?

2. If your inner critic has been telling you one story, it's time you rewrite the ending. What is one of those stories you keep hearing?

Day 56

GIVING TO OURSELVES

That word *selfish* comes up all the time when I talk with women about making room for ourselves. We are taught by society—by our upbringing—to be givers. We give, we give, we give, and we feel guilty taking.

You might be wrestling with this concept of giving space and time to yourself because it challenges so much of what you know about who you are and your role in this world.

You are a giver, I know. You love to give to others, even at the expense of yourself. If I were there next to you, I would take your hand, look you in the eye, and tell you this truth: When we make time for our wants and needs, we are able to give our fullest selves to the world around us.

The things that matter—like love, happiness, and compassion—need to be cultivated in your own life before you can make a difference in the world by extending those feelings to others. John Maxwell said it best when he reminded us, "To bring out the best in others, I first have to bring out the best in me. I cannot give what I do not have."[19] This is a mantra I often need to put on repeat in my own head.

If we don't have compassion for ourselves, how can we give it to others? If we don't love ourselves, how can we truly love others? We speak to ourselves in hurtful, angry tones. We hurl insults—things we would never say aloud to anyone else—but we think nothing of saying these poisonous words to ourselves. The grace we give to others greatly exceeds the grace we offer ourselves.

I understand that the idea of self-care can feel a little too warm and fuzzy for some people, but there's a lot of hard evidence to back it up. Studies have shown it increases our problem-solving abilities, research showing it helps us bounce back after adversity, and evidence affirms it even increases self-motivation. When we practice self-compassion, it boosts our overall satisfaction with life.

Being mindful and taking time to give yourself the space you need is an investment in yourself. I think so many women struggle with this because white space might feel like a waste of time—after all, you aren't running around and doing things. You are being still. But giving yourself white space and taking care of yourself isn't a luxury, and it's not pampering. It's essential to higher productivity, creativity, and concentration.

1. When you feel satisfied with your life, do you see the effects in all the areas of your world? How you treat your family? How you connect with friends?

2. Make a list of three to five things that would feel like self-care to you. Can you make room to do at least one of these things this week?

FINDING YOUR YES

To create the white space we need in our lives, we need to carve out that space for ourselves. We know we can't just make more time; we have to find it somewhere in our schedule. But how can we do that when our schedule is already packed full?

The seemingly obvious answer is that we need to say no more often. Simple advice, but it's not really that easy. The challenge in life is not just saying no; it's the art of learning when your answer should be a "no" and when it should be a "yes." It's about finding *your* yes.

We need to start by clearing out the clutter so we can open up spaces for our yeses. The best way for us to do that is to uncommit.

That word *uncommit* may feel a little bit like a rock in your shoe. It's uncomfortable because we worry this means we are letting others down. But what if I told you this—you are already saying no all the time. You see, every time you say yes, you are saying no to something else. Every. Single. Time. When we commit our time to others' priorities, it's at the expense of our own.

We say yes to volunteering on a committee we don't love, so we say no to time with family. We say yes to coordinating a project for a group, so we say no to our own passion project. We cannot say yes without saying no. We have to steal the time, the energy, and the focus away from somewhere—we often just don't realize it.

It feels easy to say yes, to add "one more thing." One-more-thing-itis is real. Our schedule ends up looking like a plate of food at the end of the buffet line—heaping and overflowing—with no room left for what we really want . . . dessert.

Just because you have the time doesn't mean you should say yes. We have to save room for our yeses, just like we have to save room for that dessert.

It's not just about uncommitting and saying no. You need to commit to what *is* important to you. Have the courage and confidence to make room for more of the yeses that belong to you.

1. Is it easier for you to say yes to others than it is to yourself? When you think about the idea that "every time you say yes, you are saying no to something else," what have you been saying no to?

2. Now that you are more aware of what really matters to you, what "dessert"—what yes in your life—do you want to save room for?

Day 58

A KIND AND CONFIDENT NO

We've all heard the phrase "no is a complete sentence," and while I agree with the concept, I know it's not easy to implement in real life. Most of us don't feel comfortable with just saying no, so we end up overexplaining, overapologizing, and sometimes getting suckered into saying yes after all! The key is to make saying no easier for yourself, so you are more confident saying it.

My favorite technique to accomplish this is a simple but effective method called the Sandwich Strategy. Imagine a standard, everyday sandwich: two pieces of bread with some kind of filling nestled in the middle. When we need to say no to an opportunity, the no is the meat of our message, so we simply sandwich it in between two slices of kindness. Here's how you can use the Sandwich Strategy to say no to a request for a committee: "I am so flattered you thought of me for this important committee. Unfortunately, I have several other activities I've committed to, so I'm unable to give it the time it deserves. I am thrilled, though, that you are pulling together a group of people for such a worthwhile cause!"

Do you see the clear no right there in the middle? But because it's started and finished with compassion, it's easier to swallow. And bonus for us, it's easier to give.

There are times, too, when you'll need to give yourself some space to weigh out whether it's your yes or not. We often default to saying *maybe* or *probably*, which are soft yeses that we then feel obligated to follow through on.

Let the person requesting your time know you are seriously considering it, but it's not a soft yes: "That sounds like something I'd normally be interested in. I'm not sure I'll be able to give it the time it deserves, so I need some time to think about it. I'll let you know Friday. I really appreciate you thinking of me."

I understand there are times when you feel you cannot say no, but I promise you can. And you can do it in ways that are respectful and kind. Yes, even if it is your boss who sometimes needs to be told no.

Deliver your sandwich with positivity, calmness, and the best results you can. I'm not going to pretend saying no is easy, but when you say no, you open up opportunities for even bigger yeses.

1. Do you currently feel overcommitted? What's one thing you need to uncommit to in order to create more white space and peace of mind?

2. In thinking of that thing that you need to uncommit to, write out your Sandwich Strategy below to kindly say no.

Day 59

LETTING GO OF SOMEDAY

I have no interest in being Superwoman, but there are times when I feel compelled to try. Even worse, I sometimes feel others trying to clip that cape on my shoulders, and I start to feel the weight of it dragging me down. You have probably felt that too.

When we get caught up in focusing on what we are "supposed" to do, we find ourselves going through the motions of life rather than doing what we really want to do. We assure ourselves that someday this cycle will stop, that once certain conditions get better, everything will improve.

We tell ourselves these stories:

I need to work weekends until I make partner; then I'll have time to spend with my family.
I have so much to do. I just don't have the luxury of going out with my friends.
Someday things will be easier, and I'll get to do the things I really want.

Unfortunately, "someday" is like a mirage on the horizon; each time we get closer, it keeps moving farther and farther away. Truly, without effort on our part, nothing will change, and our priorities will continue to be put last.

When we don't take the time to actively choose how we spend our days, each task on our list feels unavoidable. It feels justifiable to postpone date night with our spouse, miss a movie with friends, or skip the gym (again). We end up putting it off, exhausted and too tired to enjoy the things we, in our heart of hearts, truly enjoy most. That's not the way we want to live.

Stop borrowing from today to make tomorrow great. Instead, let's choose to make the most of today, knowing that when we spend our days focusing on priorities, we are investing in our future.

Part of this process, too, is forgiving yourself for mistakes you've made in your life. Maybe you have run your life like a circus, and you are ready for it to stop. Maybe you have said yes far too often, or maybe you have spent so much time on other people's needs that you have forgotten who you are deep inside.

It's okay. It's not what you've done in the past that matters; it's what you do moving forward that counts.

1. Are you borrowing from today to make tomorrow great? What are a few "someday" goals you want to start accomplishing now?

2. What is one task you can prioritize for today that will help you go to bed tonight and feel successful?

EVERY DAY COUNTS

The floor of the Indian Ocean is scattered with the quiet remains of over two hundred shipwrecks that met tragic fates over the course of thousands of years. Each one could be deemed a failure, but something amazing happened as these ships settled into the deep. They transformed from ghostly hulking ships into magnificent coral reefs teeming with life—fish, sponges, clams, squid, mollusks, and eels live and thrive among these lost ships.

We need to have the same perspective about our own mistakes and failures, our stumbling blocks that have held us back in the past. Each one is an opportunity for growth, and yes, even for beauty.

This transformation to coral reefs did not happen overnight; it took time and patience before new life took hold. Your transition to living a life centered on priority will take time too. Time, patience, and energy are needed to start making the shift.

Know that change will not happen overnight and that sometimes victories are small, but take time to celebrate them and be encouraged that the life you want is out there. Give yourself grace to rediscover what makes you happy and be unapologetically you. Spend your time in ways that feel like investments—invest in relationships and activities that fulfill you. Try to let go of what does not align with your priorities and the life you truly want to live.

What I want for you is more than a productive life: I want you to have the beautiful life you deserve. Now it's up to you to go get it.

This book has been about productivity, but at its heart, it's about the choices we make: the hard choices, the easy choices, the everyday choices. Our lives are defined by choices.

And now you need to make a choice. Do you want to stay on the path you are on, or do you want to make some changes to work toward the life you want?

Take one step forward, one tiny step, each and every day. Each step of this process builds upon the last, creating a strong framework for a fulfilling life. At the heart of each of these ideas we've been adjusting our beliefs, our boundaries, and our behaviors, all of which influence our lives and affect our productivity.

Anchoring each step is priority. It is possible to live a life centered on what matters most; happiness is possible when you make every day count. You just have to choose to begin.

1. Are there some failures or mistakes on your life journey? Do you see how you grew from those times?
2. What will be your first step to make every day count from here on out?

NOTES

1. *Britannica*, "Alfred Nobel," last updated October 17, 2024, https://www
   .britannica.com/biography/Alfred-Nobel.
2. *Britannica*, "information theory," last updated October 7, 2024, https://
   www.britannica.com/science/information-theory/Applications-of-information
   -theory.
3. Orison Swett Mardin, *Life Stories of Successful Men Told by Themselves* (Boston:
   Lothrop Publishing Company, 1901), 34.
4. Mark H. McCormack, *What They Don't Teach You at Harvard Business School:
   Notes from a Street-Smart Executive* (Bantam, 1984).
5. Susan Weinschenk, "The True Cost of Multi-Tasking," *Psychology Today*,
   September 18, 2012, https://www.psychologytoday.com/us/blog/brain-wise
   /201209/the-true-cost-multi-tasking.
6. Joan Halifax, quoted in Brené Brown, *Braving the Wilderness: The Quest for
   True Belonging and the Courage to Stand Alone* (Random House, 2017), 148.
7. Bob Sullivan, "Memo to Work Martyrs: Long Hours Make You Less
   Productive," CNBC, January 26, 2015, https://www.cnbc.com/2015/01/26
   /working-more-than-50-hours-makes-you-less-productive.html.
8. Henriette Anne Klauser, *Write It Down, Make It Happen: Knowing What You
   Want—And Getting It!* (Scribner, 2000), chap. 1.
9. Nicole Williams, "Does Your To Do List Need a Makeover?", *LinkedIn Official
   Blog, LinkedIn*, May 22, 2012, https://www.linkedin.com/blog/member
   /archive/professional-to-do-list.
10. Ferris Jabr, "Does Thinking Really Hard Burn Calories?," *Scientific American*,
    July 18, 2012, https://www.scientificamerican.com/article/thinking-hard
    -calories/.
11. David T. Neal, Wendy Wood, and Jeffrey M. Quinn, "Habits—A Repeat
    Performance," *Current Directions in Psychological Science* 15, no. 4 (2006):
    198–202, https://doi.org/10.1111/j.1467-8721.2006.00435.x.

12. Charles Duhigg, *The Power of Habit: Why We Do What We Do in Life and Business* (Random House, 2012).

13. Duhigg, *Power of Habit*, 283.

14. *Merriam-Webster Dictionary*, s.v. "hustle," accessed February 14, 2019, https://www.merriam-webster.com/dictionary/hustle.

15. Ernest Hemingway, "The Art of Fiction No. 21," interview by George Plimpton, *Paris Review*, no. 18 (Spring 1958): https://www.theparisreview.org/interviews/4825/the-art-of-fiction-no-21-ernest-hemingway.

16. Shawn Achor. "The Happiness Advantage: Linking Positive Brains to Performance." TED Talk, Bloomington, IL, June 30, 2011. 12 min., 29 sec. https://www.youtube.com/watch?v=GXy__kBVq1M.

17. Laura Vanderkam, *I Know How She Does It: How Successful Women Make the Most of Their Time* (Portfolio Penguin, 2015), 72.

18. "Great White Naps for First Time on Camera," posted June 28, 2016, by Discovery, YouTube, 2:33 mins., https://www.youtube.com/watch?v=B7ePdi1McMo.

19. John Maxwell expands on this concept in "Executive Leadership Podcast #3: You Cannot Give What You Do Not Have," posted April 25, 2018, by The John Maxwell Company, 15:33 mins., https://corporatesolutions.johnmaxwell.com/podcast/executive-leadership-podcast-3-you-cannot-give-what-you-do-not-have/.

ABOUT THE AUTHOR

Tanya Dalton is a bestselling author, motivational speaker, and nationally recognized productivity expert who empowers executives and entrepreneurs to embrace intentional leadership.

Her influential books have been translated into eight languages, including *The Joy of Missing Out*, named a "Top 10 Business Book of the Year" by *Fortune* magazine. Tanya's podcast, *The Intentional Advantage*, boasts millions of downloads worldwide. She's been featured as an expert on NBC, Fox, and *The Today Show*, where she shares her insights on purposeful productivity.

Tanya is also the founder of inkWELL Press Productivity Co., a multimillion-dollar company providing tools that work as a catalyst in helping people do less while achieving maximum success.

Those who know her best describe Tanya simply as a mom who loves her family fiercely, isn't afraid to make a fool of herself, and wants nothing more than for you to stop overthinking and start working toward the life you really want.

If you enjoyed *Purposeful Productivity*, make sure to connect with Tanya at TanyaDalton.com.